USING THE
INTERNET
Online Services,
& CD·ROMs
FOR WRITING RESEARCH AND TERM PAPERS

Edited by Charles Harmon

NEAL-SCHUMAN NETGUIDE SERIES

Neal-Schuman Publishers, Inc.
London
New York

Published by Neal-Schuman Publishers, Inc.
100 Varick Street
New York, NY 10013

Library of Congress Cataloging-in-Publication Data

Using the internet, online services, and CD-ROMs for writing research and term papers / edited by Charles Harmon.
    p.   cm. — (Neal-Schuman NetGuide series)
  Includes bibliographical references and index.
  ISBN 1-55570-238-4 (alk. paper)
    1. Report writing. 2. Dissertations, Academic. 3. Research—Databases.
4. CD ROMs. 5. Internet (Computer network)
I. Harmon, Charles. II. Series: Neal-Schuman net-guide series.
LB1047.3.U75   1996
371.2'028'12—dc20   95-51155

Contents

Preface

Researching and writing a research paper is without a doubt one of the most useful skills students learn. The process teaches students how to locate information, independently form a thesis, build a logical argument supporting that thesis, support that argument by selecting and using facts persuasively, and present a polished, well-written paper directed toward a specific audience. This process not only prepares us to participate in a democratic society but also provides us with a strong background for many career responsibilities.

Just a decade ago, learning how to find the information needed to write a research or term paper meant learning the difference among title, author, and subject cards in the card catalog and how to use a couple of periodical indexes like the *Readers' Guide*. Learning how to document information meant remembering where to put the quotation marks in an endnote or bibliography entry for a periodical article. Compared to learning how to surf the Net, download files from online services, and search the archives of an electronic discussion group, today's parents had an easier job researching topics than do today's high school students.

The good news is that today's term paper writer can write *interesting* papers on a wider variety of subjects because he or she can locate an almost unlimited amount of information on almost any conceivable subject. The resources available today extend far beyond the four walls of the public, school, or university library. Using the Internet, students can locate and correspond with experts in almost any field imaginable. Students can access parts of the Vatican Library, look at NASA documents, and download Supreme Court opinions.

Online services also offer a wealth of opportunities to students from their homes. Whether it's searching a particular commercial database, using Prodigy's Homework Helper, or checking a definition in an online dictionary, students are no longer limited to expensive reference books their parents might or might not be able to provide them. For less than $10 a month, a whole realm of almost limitless information can come onto a student's PC over the home telephone line.

Perhaps the most valuable part of the whole process is learning to examine and make judgments about the accuracy and applicability of the sources you have retrieved. While traditional reference works have customarily gone through an intensive review and verification process, electronic resources—especially the Internet and Web ones—may be literally the collected and posted ramblings of one individual. Learning to evaluate sources for authenticity, authority, and currency—as well as knowing how to cite electronic sources—is an essential step to becoming an information-literate person.

Using the Internet, Online Services, and CD-ROMs for Writing Research and Term Papers is designed as a practical, easy-to-follow guide combining the best of two traditional generic texts: "how to write a paper" and "how to use a library." Contributors include college English professors who discuss the writing, note-taking, outlining, and proofreading process as well as librarians and professional writers from across the country who write on their various specialties: online services, the Internet, CD-ROMs, traditional library resources, and documentation methodologies.

Using the Internet, Online Services, and CD-ROMs for Writing Research and Term Papers is organized into sections that parallel the research and writing processes. Readers follow two students, Kristen and Zak, as they choose a topic; conduct research; and write, revise, and polish their final papers, which are presented in Chapter Seven.

- Chapter One, "Getting Ready to Write and Conducting Primary Research," covers selecting a topic, setting up a schedule for researching and writing a paper, and conducting primary research such as surveys and personal observations.

- Chapter Two, "Secondary Research Using Print Sources," covers library resources such an encyclopedias, almanacs, online and card catalogs, electronic and print periodical indexes, and contains essential tips about gathering your information for maximum efficiency in using it.

- Chapter Three, "Secondary Research Using CD-ROMs," describes CD-ROMs that are commonly purchased for home use as well as those more frequently found in libraries. Journal indexes, the type of CD-ROM most heavily used for research purposes, are described in depth. Searching and printing tips and screen shots are presented for the three CD-ROM indexes most likely to be held by libraries used by students: the *Readers' Guide to Periodical Literature*, the *Expanded Academic Index* (also called *InfoTrac*), and *ProQuest*.

- Chapter Four, "Secondary Research Using Online Services," contains detailed tips for maximizing the use of the three major online services: America Online, CompuServe, and Prodigy. Both descriptions of and direction for using databases, encyclopedias, and other reference tools available through these three services are covered with examples using common research topics. This information will enable students to save both time and money. Information about each service's Internet gateway is also provided.

- Chapter Five, "Secondary Research Using the Internet," begins with a discussion of what the Internet is, how to get access to it, and what you can do on the Internet. This is followed by a detailed discussion of the major Internet resources like Gophers and the World Wide Web. Tips for locating, downloading, and printing information are given. Addresses and descriptions of major sites that are most likely to be helpful for research purposes are also provided. Twenty screen shots illustrating major points enhance the very practical information presented.

- Chapter Six, "Examining Sources, Writing, and Revising," describes what to do once you've picked a topic (Chapter One) and completed your primary (also Chapter One) and secondary (Chapters Two through Five) research. The chapter covers evaluating the sources, taking notes (in both manual and electronic formats), and using quotations. Clear, step-by-step instructions help readers choose a preliminary thesis, design an outline, and move from writing the first draft through the revision process. Examples are provided to illustrate each step.

- Chapter Seven, "Proofreading and Preparing the Final Copy," discusses the proofreading stage. It points out the benefits and shortcomings of electronic spelling and grammar checkers as well as provides tips for catching common errors. Detailed requirements for producing a finished paper conforming to MLA guidelines are accompanied by two model essays illustrating thesis statements, major arguments, references, and bibliographic form.

- Chapter Eight, "Citing Print and Electronic Sources," covers the two most commonly used styles for citing sources: the APA (American Psychological Association) and MLA (Modern Language Association). Formats and examples are given for citing information gathered from print, CD-ROM, online, and Internet resources using both styles.

The authors and editor hope that you find this a concise, helpful guide to writing research papers in the Information Age.

Charles Harmon

Chapter 1

Getting Ready to Write and Conducting Primary Research

Katherine H. Adams and John L. Adams

When journalists go to the scene of a murder, they ask questions of witnesses and examine the area. At the same time, police collect evidence and medical examiners begin to inspect the body.

These people are "re-searchers," meaning that they search and search again to get a complete picture and thus to determine the time of death, type of weapon, and ultimately the identity of the murderer. Such observation and analysis skills are also crucial to the doctor examining a patient, the sociologist observing a community, and the scientist conducting an experiment. To conduct thorough studies and form conclusions, these professionals rely on their own experience and knowledge and on primary research like observations, interviews, and surveys as well as on secondary research from textbooks, articles, and legal documents.

In your classes, teachers assign research and term papers to help you develop research skills and learn to communicate the results of your work to various audiences. The following sections will help you to choose and narrow a topic for a research paper, to decide on an outline, to write, and to revise. As we proceed, we will review the work of two students, Kristen Hubbard and Zak Cernoch, as examples of the research process.

Schedule for a Research Project

complete by

_____ 1. Decide on a general topic and narrow it. (pp. 2–4)

_____ 2. Consider the needs of your readers. (p. 4)

_____ 3. Consider your own knowledge and opinions on the topic. (p. 5)

_____ 4. Locate appropriate primary and secondary sources. (pp. 5–109)

_____ 5. Examine the arguments presented in these sources. (pp. 111–114)

_____ 6. Choose a preliminary thesis and organization. (pp. 114–116)

_____ 7. Write a rough draft. (p. 117)

_____ 8. Incorporate source materials into your arguments. (pp. 118–124)

_____ 9. Make the necessary revisions. (pp. 124–125)

_____ 10. Proofread your work and prepare the final copy (pp. 127–144).

PREWRITING

The first step in the research process is to decide on a topic and conduct research concerning it, a step called *prewriting* since this work takes place before you write a rough draft. This beginning step is perhaps the most important one because a research paper, whether it concerns AIDS, Shakespeare, careers, or capital punishment, must present specific information and an interpretation of it.

Choosing and Narrowing Your Topic

You will first need to decide on a topic you can research and write about successfully. The following suggestions will help you make your choice:

1. Pick a topic that interests you or a question you would like to answer.
You will enjoy the process more and put more work into your paper if you choose a subject or question that you want to pursue.

In his civics class, Zak heard a lecture about the death penalty. The speaker, Sister Helen Prejean, provided data about its costs and its failure to deter crime and described her experiences visiting with the men on Louisiana's death row. When his English teacher assigned a research paper a few days later, Zak decided to use this opportunity to find out more about capital punishment.

If you need help deciding on an appropriate and interesting topic, ask your teacher for ideas; browse the subject headings in your library's online or card catalog or in periodical indexes; review course readings. Try to avoid settling for an "oh, I guess this will have to do" type of topic.

2. Choose a topic *you* can research.

When you have decided on a general topic, go to the library to see whether you can find enough material on it. If the information has appeared only in journals that your library doesn't own (or is not available electronically in sources you have access to), if the topic is very new, or if everyone else in the class is writing on the same subject, you may not be able to find enough data. Ask a librarian if you need help with evaluating a possible topic.

3. Pick a topic that is sufficiently narrowed or limited.

If there are entire books on your topic, it may be too broad for a short paper.

Kristen wanted to write on television violence, but she realized that this general topic might be too much to handle, so she considered these more specific choices:

- one Saturday morning lineup or show
- shows aimed at very young children
- toys that enable children to imitate Power Rangers or other favorite cartoon heroes
- the portrayal of boys and girls in adventure cartoons
- attitudes of parents toward violent programming
- immediate effects of viewing television violence

Like Kristen, you may find that scanning book and article titles at the library can help you decide on a specific topic.

Considering Your Readers

As part of your choice of topic, you should consider the readers of the paper. Will they be your classmates or some other group?

The following questions will help you assess their knowledge and opinions:

- What age are my readers?
- How much education do they have?
- What do they value most?
- What do they fear?
- Will they be seeking my information or will I have to convince them of its importance?
- How do they feel about my topic? How does it affect them?
- How much do they know about it?
- What vocabulary concerning it will they already know?
- Will their definitions agree with mine?
- What examples will they find most disturbing or inspiring?

Carefully considering the readers' knowledge and biases will enable you to produce a paper that will be convincing to them.

Kristen Hubbard, for example, decided to address an audience of parents on the effects during childhood of repeated viewing of violent television. She thought that parents might compare watching crime shows to playing cops and robbers, a violent play activity of their own childhoods, and thus think of television viewing as being relatively harmless. She decided that she would address this opinion directly in her paper.

Sometimes you will be writing for a more general audience or for the teacher. In these situations you still should consider the readers' needs and interests carefully. A general audience (such as teachers) will generally have the following traits:

- They have a general knowledge of politics, history, entertainment, and other fields, but you should not expect them to be experts on your specific subject. Thus you will need to define specialized terminology, explain the historical background of a problem, or summarize the plot of a story.
- They will consider your thesis and supporting evidence carefully and critically.
- They appreciate clear, correct writing.

CONDUCTING THE RESEARCH

Once you have decided on a topic, careful "re-search" will enable you to increase your knowledge and prepare to address a reader. This process generally involves *personal*, *primary*, and *secondary* research.

Personal Research: Experiences You Have Had, Information You Know

Before you begin talking to other people and reading about your topic, consider what you know already. Treat yourself as the first source by jotting down answers to these questions:

- How did I first hear about this topic?
- What judgments have I already made about it? On what evidence?
- What experiences have I had or heard about that concern it?
- What have I read about this subject?
- How do my family, friends, and teachers feel about it?

After you begin working with other sources, you may need to return to these questions—to see if you are changing your mind, if you have begun to interpret your experiences differently.

When Zak answered these questions, he realized that he had always supported capital punishment, but he had based his judgment not on data, but on his feeling that a murder should be revenged. He realized that this emotional response might be shared by his readers—other college-age voters—who could also profit from a more careful consideration of the issue.

Primary Research

Another important research form is primary research, which involves learning by watching what people say and do, asking them questions, and drawing your own conclusions. Primary research methods include *observation*, *interviews*, and *surveys*.

Observation. You should learn to evaluate a situation by analyzing what you observe. To write about hospital care or shopping malls, go out and see what is going on. To write about weight lifting, don't just go to the library: visit a gym.

Before you make an observation, decide on the purpose of the session.

Kristen planned to watch cartoons with her younger brothers (ages five and seven) to consider how frequently various types of violent acts occurred, how they reacted to the violence, and how well they comprehended what they had seen. To get this information, she decided to use several viewing sessions and ask them a few questions afterwards.

When you are making such an observation, try to write everything down. You should wait until you organize a rough draft to decide on the importance of your material.

Interviews. Many people may be able to give you a firsthand account of a place or experience relevant to your topic or share their own reading with you. Ask teachers, friends, and librarians for names of such people.

When you have chosen an individual you would like to interview, contact him or her, explain your project, and request an appointment. You also might ask if you can bring a tape recorder with you.

Before the session, research your topic and the person you are interviewing. Then you won't waste time asking questions that you could easily find the answers to elsewhere. Next, with the purpose of your interview clearly in mind, prepare a short list of questions or topics.

When Kristen decided to interview a local child psychologist, Dr. Erin Broussard, who was studying television violence, she chose to ask the following questions:

1. On which cartoons do you find the most violence? What age children are they aimed at?
2. Do violent cartoons, dramas, and news shows affect children differently?
3. Do many children repeat the acts that they see on television? Do any particular types or ages of children tend to do so more frequently? Does more frequent viewing lead to more of these acts?
4. Does viewing violence make children afraid?
5. Does constant viewing of quickly moving, violent shows lessen their ability to understand complex problems and consider appropriate solutions?

Surveys. To get information from a larger group, like students and teachers at your school, you might decide to create a short survey. Although you could mail these forms, an easier method is to simply hand them out where the group is—to parents at a day care center, to children in their preschool class, or to teachers at a faculty meeting—after explaining your purpose for collecting the information.

To conduct a successful survey, you will need to choose clear and direct questions that will elicit the data you need. Before you administer the survey to your target group, test it on several classmates or members of your target audience to see if their interpretation of each question matches with your own.

Your first questions might identify the respondents by age, job, or gender, whatever information seems important to you. The additional questions, which should not take up more than a page, should be designed so that your respondents don't have to do much writing and so that you can analyze their answers easily: you might use check-off lists, five-point scales, and yes-no questions. At the end of the survey, you can include one or two questions that require a written answer if you want to encourage respondents to express more of their own viewpoints.

To find out what his fellow students thought about capital punishment, Zak designed the following survey:

Capital Punishment Survey

male _____   female _____

1. Do you support capital punishment?

    _____ yes   _____ no

2. If you support capital punishment, for what crimes do you think it should be a possible punishment? (Check all those that apply.)

    _____murder of one person
    _____multiple murders
    _____rape
    _____drug dealing
    _____other   Please state:

    _____

3. If you support capital punishment, what are your reasons for doing so? (Place a number by all those that apply, using (1) for your primary reason and then proceeding with 2, 3, etc.)

    _____It offers the only possibility for the punishment to equal the crime.
    _____It deters crime.
    _____It is less expensive than life in prison.
    _____It makes our community safer since the criminal cannot escape or be paroled.
    _____other   Please state:

    _____

4. Do you think that the poor and minorities are more likely than other groups to be sentenced to death?

    _____ yes   _____ no

5. What would you most like to tell your classmates about capital punishment?

    _____
    _____

After collecting the responses, Zak could look at many different issues: whether the students supported capital punishment and why, what information they knew, how males and females differed.

When he reported the data in his essay, he had to state exactly what he had learned: "A recent survey I conducted indicated that 79% of 105 male and female students viewed the death penalty as appropriate for murderers, of one person or of several. A much lower number, under 10%, viewed it as appropriate for any other crime." He could also quote from the written responses if he indicated that he was citing one opinion.

Secondary Research

Your secondary research will uncover most of the information for supporting your thesis as well as consume most of the time you spend on your paper before you get ready to write. Secondary research using printed sources is discussed in the following chapter. Chapter 3 discusses using CD-ROMs to unearth secondary information, Chapter 4 is devoted to online services, and, finally, Chapter 5 discusses the wealth of information available on the Internet and the World Wide Web.

Choosing which kind of source to use and when is an important consideration that shouldn't be overlooked. Obviously, it's a lot more likely that you'll find yesterday's news in either a newspaper, on American Online, or on the Net than it is that you'll find it on a CD-ROM. Likewise, it's unlikely that an online service is going to include information on obscure eighteenth-century painters. Think carefully about the attributes of each kind of source before you spend time using it. If you're in doubt about where is the best place to look after reading the descriptions of these sources and how to use them in the following chapters, ask a librarian.

Chapter 2

Secondary Research Using Print Sources

Katherine H. Adams and John L. Adams

As you collect appropriate types of primary data, you should also turn to printed materials, called secondary sources.

The following sections—on reference works, books, and periodical articles—will help you to use printed sources in the library effectively.

FINDING BACKGROUND INFORMATION IN REFERENCE WORKS

You should locate several overviews of your subject in reference books. The reference room of your library contains many valuable sources that provide background information and statistical data on almost every subject. You can locate these research tools by finding your topic in the online or card catalog and then looking under the subheading "Dictionaries"; by using the *Guide to Reference Books* (11th edition, edited by Robert Balay), a source that lists 10,000 reference books by subject area; or by asking a librarian.

The following sections will acquaint you with some of the most helpful reference tools.

Encyclopedias

You can often find information in general encyclopedias like *Collier's Encyclopedia, Encyclopedia Americana*, and *The New Encyclopaedia Britannica*, which are written for a general audience and cover a wide variety of subjects. But the reference room also contains encyclopedias devoted to specific fields. These specialized encyclopedias, like the ones listed here, provide more detailed background information, an overview of current debates, and bibliographies:

> *Encyclopedia of Advertising*
> *Encyclopedia of Computer Science and Technology*
> *Encyclopedia of Crime and Justice*
> *Encyclopedia of Education*
> *Encyclopedia of Electronics*
> *Encyclopedia of Psychology*
> *Encyclopedia of World Art*
> *McGraw-Hill Encyclopedia of Science and Technology*
> *McGraw-Hill Encyclopedia of World Drama*

Encyclopedias are also available online and in CD-ROM formats. See the following chapters for information on choosing and using these.

Biographical Dictionaries

Biographical reference works contain brief accounts of well-known figures. To find information about the people who played significant roles in the events you are studying, you might look them up in the following biographical sources:

> *Current Biography* covers persons of various nationalities and professions, providing a biographical sketch, short bibliography, picture (with some entries), and address.
>
> *Dictionary of American Biography* contains short biographies of over 15,000 deceased Americans representing many professions.
>
> *Who's Who in America, Who's Who* (primary British), and *The International Who's Who* offer brief biographies of notable living people. The "who's who" label has also been used on a variety of other biographical sources:
>
> > *Who's Who Among Black Americans*
> > *Who's Who in American Art*

Who's Who in American Education
Who's Who in American Politics
Who's Who in Economics
Who's Who in Hollywood, 1900–1976
Who's Who in Horror and Fantasy Fiction
Who's Who in Military History
Who's Who in Rock
Who's Who in Television and Cable

Almanacs

For the facts and statistics necessary to substantiate your claims, almanacs are an invaluable source. Their tables, charts, lists, and thorough indexes give the researcher quick access to all kinds of data. Here are two examples:

The World Almanac and Book of Facts. This reference tool contains such diverse facts as the names of sports champions, college tuition costs, and execution totals by state. The almanac covers historical as well as current information.

Statistical Abstracts of the United States. Published by the U.S. Bureau of the Census, this book contains information gathered each year under such categories as Health and Nutrition; Education; Geography and Environment; and Communications.

Dictionaries

The library's unabridged dictionaries enable you to check the meaning of key terms. The *Oxford English Dictionary* explains the derivation of words and their meanings in earlier centuries. Specialized dictionaries, like those in the following list, cover the specialized terminology of particular fields or careers:

Dictionary of Computer Terms
Dictionary of Concepts in General Psychology
Dictionary of Criminal Justice
Dictionary of Ecology
Dictionary of Film and Broadcast Terms
Dictionary of Geography
Dictionary of Historical Terms

Dictionary of Legal Terms
Dictionary of Money and Finance
Dictionary of Music
A Dictionary of Politics
A Dictionary of Science Terms
Dictionary of Television, Cable, and Video

SEARCHING FOR BOOKS

After you have looked in various reference works to get an overview of your topic—and perhaps to narrow it further—you will be ready to use other types of books and periodicals to find more detailed information.

The following steps will help you locate relevant data in library books.

Find the Subject Headings for Your Topic

You will waste time and miss sources if you head straight to the online or card catalog, trusting in your own label for the topic. You first need to consult the *Library of Congress Subject Headings,* found in book form or on microfiche near the online catalog in your library. This guide will tell you what subject headings to use.

If Kristen planned to look under "television violence" or "violence on television," for example, she would find that these labels are not used in online catalogs. Instead, she would need to look under "violence in television." She could also use broader terms like "television programs" and "violence in mass media" as well as narrower terms like "crime in television."

Use the Online or Card Catalog

After choosing the correct subject terms, you will be ready to use the online or card catalog and create a list of books that seem likely to contain information on your topic. If your library's online system is new, all of the older books may not be listed on it. Ask a librarian if you will need to use the card drawers to search for older books.

The catalog lists books by author, title, and subject heading. For most searches, you will be relying on the subject heading entries, which begin with Library of Congress subject headings.

You can save time—and find the best materials—if you study the entries carefully. Each card or computer entry, like the sample given here, contains a great deal of information that should help you decide whether to choose a book or not.

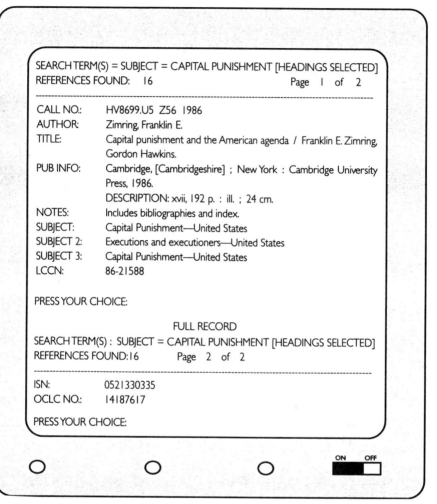

SEARCH TERM(S) = SUBJECT = CAPITAL PUNISHMENT [HEADINGS SELECTED]
REFERENCES FOUND: 16   Page 1 of 2

CALL NO.:   HV8699.U5 Z56 1986
AUTHOR: Zimring, Franklin E.
TITLE: Capital punishment and the American agenda / Franklin E. Zimring,
               Gordon Hawkins.
PUB INFO: Cambridge, [Cambridgeshire] ; New York : Cambridge University
               Press, 1986.
               DESCRIPTION: xvii, 192 p. : ill. ; 24 cm.
NOTES: Includes bibliographies and index.
SUBJECT: Capital Punishment—United States
SUBJECT 2:   Executions and executioners—United States
SUBJECT 3:   Capital Punishment—United States
LCCN: 86-21588

PRESS YOUR CHOICE:

                              FULL RECORD
SEARCH TERM(S) : SUBJECT = CAPITAL PUNISHMENT [HEADINGS SELECTED]
REFERENCES FOUND:16   Page 2 of 2

ISN: 0521330335
OCLC NO.:   14187617

PRESS YOUR CHOICE:

ON   OFF

Figure 1-1.   In addition to the book's call number, library catalog entries contain lots of other information that can help you find additional information sources.

Here are some of the questions you should ask about each potential source. You may not be able to answer all of them, but the answers you generate will help you decide whether the book will be worth locating:

- **Author's name:** Do you know who the author is? Have you read or seen entries for other books by the author? Is he or she a well-known expert? Franklin E. Zimring, for example, is a professor of law and director of a legal institute at the University of California, Berkeley.

- **Title:** Does the title seem related to your topic? The words "American agenda" in this title perhaps indicate that the book will explore the reasons that the United States continues to employ capital punishment when all other Western industrial nations have abandoned it.
- **Date of publication:** When was the book published? If a book about television appeared in the 1960s, for example, it may provide interesting historical data but not the latest findings. This book's publication date of 1986 indicates that it will not include data on recent executions or public opinion.
- **Page numbers and inclusions:** You might want to note the length of the book and whether it contains illustrations, a bibliography, and an index.
- **Subject headings:** You should also note the other subject headings under which the book is listed because they may lead you to additional books on your topic. This book is listed under two subject headings besides "Capital punishment."

If you are using an online catalog, you may also be able to find out whether a book has been checked out.

Even if you need only three or four sources, record or print the information about every book that seems relevant to your topic. You will save time when you begin looking for books if you have a long list of choices.

SEARCHING FOR PERIODICAL AND NEWSPAPER ARTICLES

While you are finding relevant books, you should also search for pertinent material from magazines or journals. "Magazine" refers to *Newsweek*, *Sports Illustrated*, and other general reader periodicals that might be sold at a newsstand. Journals—like the *Journal of Social Issues* or *The New England Journal of Medicine*—contain scholarly articles intended for experts. Both types are called periodicals.

You should look for periodical articles because they contain recent scholarship about very specific subjects. By checking both magazines and journals, you can choose articles aimed at different readers and thus obtain various perspectives on a topic. For a daily news perspective, you might also want to use stories from major newspapers.

Use Periodical Indexes (Both Printed and Computerized)

To find periodical articles on your subject, you will need to use an index. The *Readers' Guide to Periodical Literature*, which you have probably used before, primarily lists magazine articles under Library of Congress subject headings.

To locate more detailed, scholarly articles, you will want to use specialized indexes, also found in the library's reference room. Many of them look like *Readers' Guide*, but they contain entries from journals in one specific field. Some specialized indexes also have short summaries, or abstracts. The following list will give you an idea of the specialized indexes that are available:

America: History and Life
Art Index
Biological Abstracts
Business Periodicals Index
Criminal Justice Periodicals Index
Communications Abstracts
The Education Index
General Science Index
Humanities Index
Index Medicus
*MLA International Bibliography of Books and Articles on the Modern
    Languages and Literatures*
Music Index
Social Sciences Index

With printed indexes, you have to look for your topic in each annual volume. But some of these indexes are also available online, allowing you to search several titles at once for articles published over several years and print out the bibliographic information and abstracts for what you find.

Most libraries have periodical databases on CD-ROM (Compact Disc, Read-Only Memory) that are updated regularly. If your library has Wilsondisc, you can search any of the H.W. Wilson indexes, like *Readers' Guide, Humanities Index, Social Sciences Index,* or *Business Periodicals Index.* Your library may also have InfoTrac I or II, which indexes business, technical, legal, and general periodicals as well as the *New York Times.* (Chapter 3 covers CD-ROM sources in detail.)

In addition to CD-ROMs, many libraries also provide access to computer networks linked by telephone connections. The Internet is a huge network linking libraries, businesses, the government, and individuals, enabling you to gain immediate access to indexes and online journals. DIALOG Information Retrieval Service, an information service, allows you to use more than 300 indexes. Other popular computer databases are ORBIT, BRS Information Technologies, and Mead Data Central. Ask your librarian to help you with these online services and to explain any charges that you may incur in using them. (Chapters 4 and 5 provide additional information on online services and the Internet.)

Whether you find entries through a computerized or a paper index, you will want to examine them carefully, by looking at the author, the title of the article, the title of the periodical, the length of the article, the date, and certainly an abstract if one is available. You should also find out whether your library receives the periodical and what call number it is listed under: libraries either provide a printed list of their periodical holdings or include entries for their periodicals on the online catalog.

Check Newspaper Indexes

Newspapers provide day-to-day accounts of historical events. Their editorial and "Living" sections can also acquaint you with the opinions and habits of earlier eras and different places. Most major newspapers, like the *New York Times* and the *Washington Post*, have printed and online indexes.

GATHERING YOUR SOURCES

With a preliminary bibliography compiled, you will be ready to locate your sources. You can check in the lobby or the reference room of the library to see what call numbers are found on what floors. Newer issues of some magazines and newspapers may be in a reading room; some of the older ones may be on microfilm.

Here are a few tips that can save you time when you are collecting materials:

1. **Make sure that each source has information that is relevant to your topic.** Before you check out a book or copy an article, do a bit of prereading. First, check the book's index to make sure that it contains information on your topic. Then quickly scan the cited pages to decide whether the information is relevant. You can

then take home—or photocopy pages from—only those books that will be helpful. Similarly, you might scan a periodical article or study its abstract and introduction before deciding to copy it or read the entire piece. Also check to see if these sources mention other ones that you might want to locate.

2. **Browse the shelves near the books you have come to get.** Since books are shelved by subjects, the ones nearby may also be pertinent to your topic.

3. **Plan for documentation.** If you photocopy parts of articles or books, write down the publication information (author, title, date, publisher, volume, and page numbers) on the copy itself and staple the pages together. Then you will have this information when you begin compiling a list of sources. (See Chapter 8 for help with documentation.)

Chapter 3

Secondary Research Using CD-ROMs

Sarah Sheehan-Harris

Everyone knows about CDs. They play music or games. You may even have used one to find an encyclopedia article. CD-ROMs are great tools for secondary research because they allow you to search in ways that would be impossible with printed sources. CD-ROMs found in libraries today includes ones filled with poetry, magazine and newspaper articles, journal indexes, paintings from the world's great museums, and even sports statistics. This chapter will look primarily at the two kinds of CD-ROMs most commonly used by students writing research papers: electronic reference books and journal indexes.

ELECTRONIC REFERENCE BOOKS

Many standard library resources—encyclopedias, dictionaries, and handbooks—are now being produced on CD-ROM. These are basic reference sources you would find in the reference room of your school or local library. Many of these require a multimedia computer in order for the user to benefit from features like moving pictures and sound. If you've purchased a new computer recently with a CD-ROM player it probably came with several CD-ROMs. Usually these are popular items like games, but if an encyclopedia was included, you now own your first electronic research tool.

One of the major drawbacks with using an electronic reference tool, especially a dictionary or encyclopedia, is it may take you some time to figure out how it works. Unlike a book, which usually is set up alphabetically and allows you to flip through until you find what you need, a CD-ROM utilizes commands you must learn to find your information. Also, you must spell your search terms correctly, because most CD-ROMs are unable to provide a standardized list of search terms. Or if they do provide search terms, the terms may not be what you would actually call the subject. Overall, though, the benefits do outweigh any drawbacks the CD-ROMs might have.

CD-ROM encyclopedias are great. They contain the actual article from an encyclopedia as well as wonderful graphics and in many cases video images and sound. Using the *New Grolier's Multimedia Encyclopedia* or the *Encarta Multimedia Encyclopedia* by Microsoft you can see and hear John F. Kennedy deliver his inaugural address instead of just reading it. Or you can see a picture of the pyramids in Egypt, instead of reading about them in a book. Also, CD-ROM encyclopedias can be less expensive than a complete book-set encyclopedia, so many students are more likely to have their own copy and more libraries can have one for their students.

Dictionaries on CD-ROM are also very popular. The *Oxford English Dictionary* and the *American Heritage Talking Dictionary* are the ones most likely to be found in libraries. A dictionary on CD-ROM will incorporate more graphics, just like an encyclopedia. CD-ROM dictionaries often include the correct pronunciation of words, accessible if your computer workstation has a sound card. In reality, though, you can usually find the information just as fast using a traditional book dictionary.

One thing CD-ROMs can do is link information together. One of the best examples is the *Software Toolworks U.S. Atlas.* The atlas can display a map of an individual state, with a different screen for a map of the topography, like most print atlases. But this atlas can also list statistics on agriculture, crime, economics, population, and much more. And statistics are great additions to your research paper, because they can dramatically support your thesis. This atlas also can provide pictures of scenic areas and major cities in the states. This resource brings together facts that you would have to search through many different books to find.

Most of the above resources are fairly standard tools found in larger offices and some homes. But these next resources are usually found only in libraries.

The *Gale Literary Index* is a comprehensive list of authors from Gale's

Contemporary Authors series, *Twentieth Century Literary Criticism, Dictionary of Literary Biography,* and many others. If you are working on a research paper and need background information about an author or critical analysis of two works of literature, this would be a very good place to start your research—and one of the best resources for any English paper.

The federal government issues many statistical resources on CD-ROM, including the *Statistical Abstract of the United States* and the *City-County Databook.* These two resources will give any number of vital statistics about people in the U.S. and how we live our lives. But they can be very complicated to use. If you want to include statistics in your paper, your best bet is to check with your librarian for help using these CD-ROMs.

JOURNAL INDEXES

The type of CD-ROM that will help you the most in writing a research paper is a journal index. A journal index will list magazine articles on a particular subject and tell you what magazine the article is in. This is much faster than searching through fifty-two issues of *Time* magazine for an article you thought you read a couple of months ago. Journal indexes list citations: the title and author of the article, and the name, page numbers, and date of the journal. A citation from the popular journal index *Readers' Guide to Periodical Literature* (the big green books found in most libraries) looks like this:

Monster on the loose: REM opens tour in Australia. D. Fricke. il Rolling Stone p27+ Mr 23 '95.

First is the title of the article, then the author of the article. The term "il" means that there is an illustration along with the article. The journal is *Rolling Stone* magazine and the article starts on page 27. A + means that the article is longer than just that page. Finally, the date of the journal issue is given.

Journal indexes on CD-ROM can be faster and easier to use compared to print indexes. A single CD-ROM can hold the equivalent of approximately 200,000 pages. That means that more than one year of journal article citations can be found on a single CD-ROM index, whereas you would have to search several volumes of a print index to cover the same time span. Though using a CD-ROM index may initially be more challenging, ultimately the technology yields both savings in time and more comprehensive results.

Also, in many CD-ROM indexes you won't find just the citation to an article; you will also find an abstract. An abstract is a summary of the article. Using an index that has abstracts can be very helpful, because when you read the article summary you know what the article is about and whether or not it will be helpful to your research.

There are a lot of different CD-ROM journal indexes available and not all libraries can afford to buy all of them. But most libraries will have a general subject index on CD-ROM, which is a good place to start your research. You won't be able to search every CD-ROM index the same way, so if you need to use different CD-ROM indexes allow yourself some extra time to familiarize yourself with new ways of searching.

As with print indexes, you'll find that your library probably doesn't own every journal listed on CD-ROM indexes. Indexes are commercial products, and they will be used at hundreds of different libraries, so not every library can own every journal indexed by them. A good rule of thumb is to find twice as many citations as you think you will need. In other words, if your instructor says you must have five journal articles for your paper, make sure you find ten appropriate citations. Then, if your library doesn't own all of the journals named in the citations, you can just go on to the next one on the list rather than having to go back to the CD-ROM workstation and repeat the search.

Usually more than one CD-ROM index is loaded on a single computer workstation. Check the top of the computer screen to make sure you are searching the index you want. Libraries will almost always place their CD-ROM index computers together. Not all computers will do the same thing in a library, so make sure you are using a workstation that will allow you to access the index you want.

Some of the most popular CD-ROM indexes are *Readers' Guide to Periodical Literature*, produced by the H. W. Wilson Company, *Expanded Academic Index* and *InfoTrac* by Information Access Company, and *Periodical Abstracts* and *ProQuest* by University Microfilms International. You don't have to remember who created these CD-ROMs, just remember the names, i.e., *Readers' Guide*. Besides general subject indexes, there are a number of subject specific indexes available from these publishers, a company called SilverPlatter, and other companies. These indexes will help you find articles for your research paper and all are different to use.

The best advice, though, if you have any questions about what types of CD-ROM indexes your library has, how to use them, or which computer has what CD-ROMs, is to ask a librarian.

Readers' Guide To Periodical Literature

Readers' Guide to Periodical Literature is the most popular general subject index in print form, and the CD-ROM version is also widely found in libraries. *Readers' Guide to Periodical Literature* is part of the Wilson family of indexes covering many subjects. When you learn to search one index from a particular CD-ROM publisher you will be able to search others on different subjects put out by the same publisher. Some of the other subject indexes published by Wilson are *Business Periodicals Index, Education Index, General Science Index,* and *Applied Science and Technology Index.*

Readers' Guide to Periodical Literature indexes 191 general interest journals. (Magazines, journals, and periodicals are all basically the same thing, so for the sake of clarity we will use the term *journal* here). Journals you would find on a newsstand, such as *Time, Newsweek, Fortune,* and *BusinessWeek,* are indexed in *Readers' Guide to Periodical Literature.* If you are not sure which journals you can use for your assignment, ask your instructor.

Using *Readers' Guide to Periodical Literature* is fairly easy. You could quickly find several hundred articles on your topic and become overwhelmed with information. When you go to the library, bring your thesis statement with you and some ideas for narrowing your topic. The following example will be for research on the topic of censorship in rock music.

To begin your search using *Readers' Guide to Periodical Literature* you will have to decide which type of search you want to do. A Single Subject Search or a Browse allows you to search one idea, such as rock music. A Multiple Subject Search allows you to search up to three subjects. Using the arrow keys, select which search you want to do.

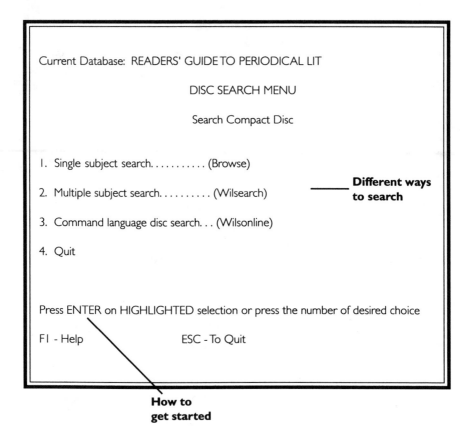

Current Database: READERS' GUIDE TO PERIODICAL LIT

DISC SEARCH MENU

Search Compact Disc

1. Single subject search. . . . . (Browse)

2. Multiple subject search. . . . . (Wilsearch)   **Different ways
                                                                to search**

3. Command language disc search. . . (Wilsonline)

4. Quit

Press ENTER on HIGHLIGHTED selection or press the number of desired choice

FI - Help   ESC - To Quit

**How to
get started**

To do a Single Subject Search on the term *rock and roll*, press the
ENTER key to make the computer start the search.

Dates covered by CD-ROM

READERS' GUIDE TO PERIODICAL LIT   Data coverage: 1/85 thru 4/95

Enter **SUBJECT** (for personal NAMEs: LAST name, FIRST name)

rock and roll

Then **PRESS ENTER - PRESS ESC** to **CANCEL**

FI = HELP   ESC = DISC SEARCH MENU

Type in subject you want to search

Readers' Guide to Periodical Literature will bring up a list of subjects in alphabetical order closest to your subject. It will also tell you the time period the CD-ROM covers in the upper right corner.

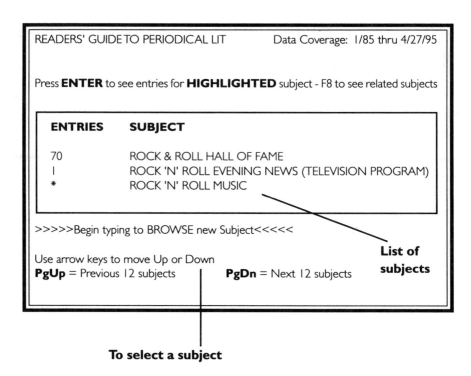

To select a subject

Rock and roll isn't in the list of subjects, so you can press the F8 key to see related subjects or use the arrow keys to highlight a different subject. The number on the left side of the entry shows how many articles are found under that subject. If there is an asterisk, it means that there are no articles.

One way that Single Subject Searching is helpful is if you are unsure of how to spell your subject. Type in your subject as best you can and the computer will pull up subjects closest in alphabetical order; you can view the entries until you find one with the correct spelling.

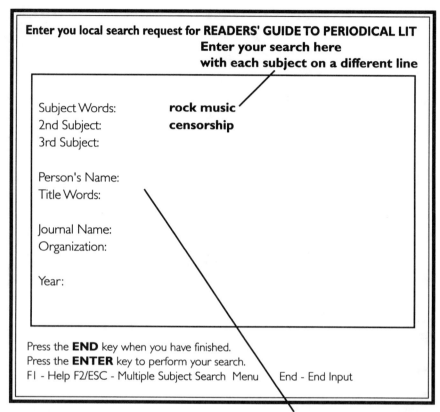

Enter you local search request for **READERS' GUIDE TO PERIODICAL LIT**
Enter your search here
with each subject on a different line

Subject Words: **rock music**
2nd Subject: **censorship**
3rd Subject:

Person's Name:
Title Words:

Journal Name:
Organization:

Year:

Press the **END** key when you have finished.
Press the **ENTER** key to perform your search.
F1 - Help F2/ESC - Multiple Subject Search Menu   End - End Input

You don't have to fill every line

The second way to search is the Multiple Subject Search. Use the arrow keys or type the number 2 to select this type of search from the first menu. Then just fill in the blanks the best you can.

Remember, you don't have to fill in each line. The line that allows you to specify the Journal Name you would like to search is helpful if you know of a specific article from a specific journal. As a rule, don't try to fill in every line, because then everything you asked for will have to be found in each article the index finds.

When you are finished filling in the lines, press the END key. That lets the computer know you have input all your information. Then press the ENTER key to make the computer perform your search.

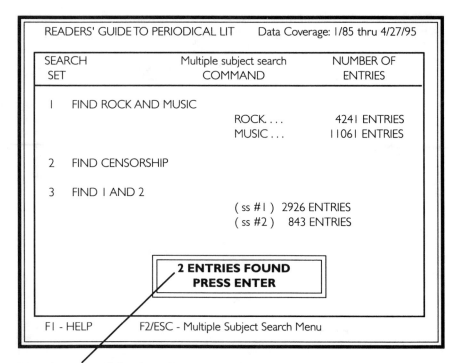

READERS' GUIDE TO PERIODICAL LIT   Data Coverage: 1/85 thru 4/27/95

SEARCH SET	Multiple subject search COMMAND	NUMBER OF ENTRIES
1 FIND ROCK AND MUSIC		
	ROCK. . . .	4241 ENTRIES
	MUSIC . . .	11061 ENTRIES
2 FIND CENSORSHIP		
3 FIND 1 AND 2		
	(ss #1) 2926 ENTRIES	
	(ss #2) 843 ENTRIES	

2 ENTRIES FOUND
PRESS ENTER

F1 - HELP   F2/ESC - Multiple Subject Search Menu

Number of articles found on your subject

This screen shows the computer searching and how many articles it found for each word. Then the computer combines all your words together and tells you how many articles it found.

To view the two articles press the ENTER key.

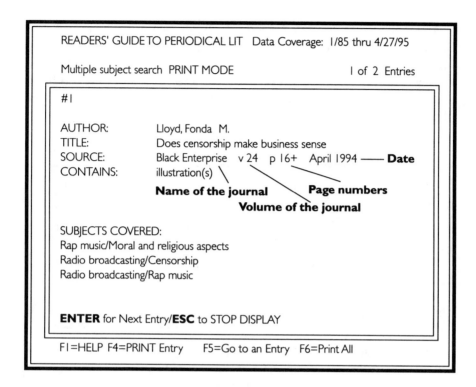

Readers' Guide to Periodical Literature LIT Data Coverage: 1/85 thru 4/27/95

Multiple subject search PRINT MODE   1 of 2 Entries

#1

AUTHOR: Lloyd, Fonda M.
TITLE: Does censorship make business sense
SOURCE: Black Enterprise   v 24   p 16+   April 1994 ——— **Date**
CONTAINS: illustration(s)
                 Name of the journal   **Page numbers**
                               Volume of the journal

SUBJECTS COVERED:
Rap music/Moral and religious aspects
Radio broadcasting/Censorship
Radio broadcasting/Rap music

ENTER for Next Entry/**ESC** to STOP DISPLAY

F1 =HELP F4=PRINT Entry   F5=Go to an Entry F6=Print All

Readers' Guide to Periodical Literature will label the author and title of the article, but the name of the journal is listed under SOURCE. Always check the SUBJECTS COVERED section to find other ideas for your topic.

The best part of using a CD-ROM index is that you can print the record: no more writer's cramp for you. To print just this citation, press the F4 key, or to print all the citations, press the F6 key as it says at the bottom of the screen. If there are more than ten citations, be selective; you don't want to be overwhelmed with paper.

Expanded Academic Index

Expanded Academic Index or *InfoTrac* is very similar to the *Readers' Guide to Periodical Literature.* You will find articles from general interest journals such as *Time* and *BusinessWeek,* but you will also find more scholarly sources like the *Chronicle of Higher Education* and the *Journal of the American Medical Association.* Articles from such authoritative, scholarly sources add weight to your paper. In other words, you'll probably get a better grade if you use a few articles from them.

You can search *Expanded Academic Index* two ways: by established Subject Guide or by Key Words. (Basically, this is the same idea as searching *Readers' Guide to Periodical Literature,* just under different terminology.) A Subject Guide search looks for a term assigned by the index such as *rock music* for *rock and roll.* Use the arrow keys to select the type of search you want to do.

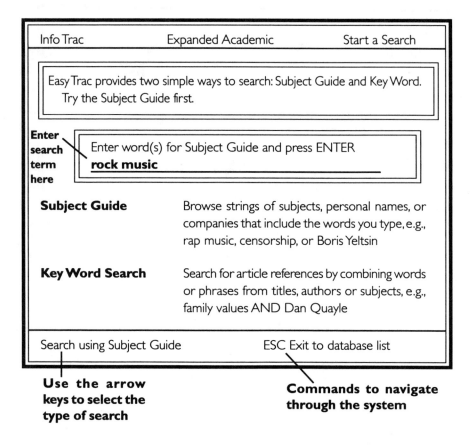

Info Trac	Expanded Academic	Start a Search

Easy Trac provides two simple ways to search: Subject Guide and Key Word. Try the Subject Guide first.

Enter search term here

Enter word(s) for Subject Guide and press ENTER
rock music

Subject Guide — Browse strings of subjects, personal names, or companies that include the words you type, e.g., rap music, censorship, or Boris Yeltsin

Key Word Search — Search for article references by combining words or phrases from titles, authors or subjects, e.g., family values AND Dan Quayle

Search using Subject Guide   ESC Exit to database list

Use the arrow keys to select the type of search

Commands to navigate through the system

When you perform a Subject Guide search in *Expanded Academic Index* you can look at the articles by that subject heading. *Expanded Academic Index* will list the subjects and how many articles are found under each subject.

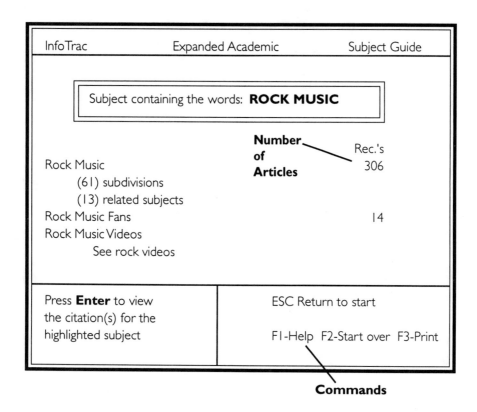

Using the arrow keys, choose a subject you are interested in and press the ENTER key. Now a list of citations will come up by date, with the most recent information first.

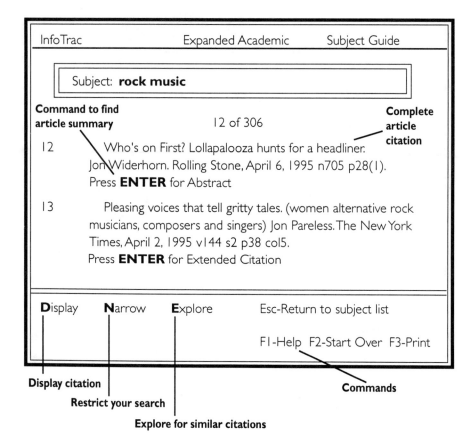

InfoTrac   Expanded Academic   Subject Guide

Subject: **rock music**

**Command to find
article summary**   12 of 306   **Complete
article
citation**

12   Who's on First? Lollapalooza hunts for a headliner.
                Jon Widerhorn. Rolling Stone, April 6, 1995 n705 p28(1).
                Press **ENTER** for Abstract

13   Pleasing voices that tell gritty tales. (women alternative rock
                musicians, composers and singers) Jon Pareless. The New York
                Times, April 2, 1995 v144 s2 p38 col5.
                Press **ENTER** for Extended Citation

Display   **N**arrow   **E**xplore   Esc-Return to subject list

                                                        F1-Help F2-Start Over F3-Print

Display citation   **Commands**

        Restrict your search

            Explore for similar citations

When you find an article you like, highlight it and press the ENTER
key to see the complete citation and an abstract of the article.

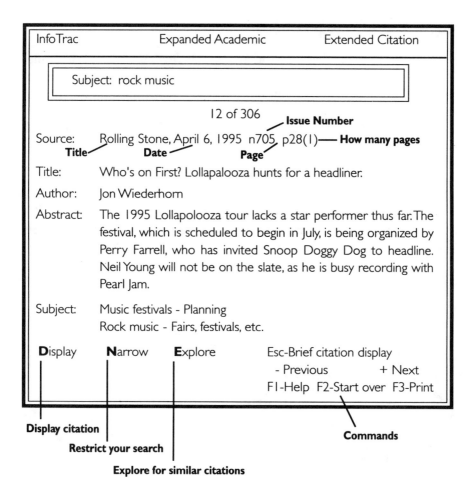

If you want to use this article in your research project, press the F3 key to print the citation or the citation with the abstract. Once you have printed the citation ask your librarian where you can find the article in the library. *Expanded Academic Index* also may contain the full text of the articles on the CD-ROM. Not all libraries have this capability, though, so check with your librarian.

When you search *Expanded Academic Index* by Key Word, the index will search for your keyword(s) in the title and abstract of the article. In a Key Word search you may search on more than one idea—e.g., censorship and rock music—and you will find articles that have both those terms.

Once *Expanded Academic Index* searches your keywords, it will list the article citations. At this point you would continue as in a Subject Guide search.

ProQuest's Periodical Abstracts

Another good database is *ProQuest's Periodical Abstracts*. It is similar in journal coverage to *Expanded Academic Index* and also contains abstracts of articles. Searches can be performed two different ways: by a list of defined Topics or subjects and by Keywords.

To begin your search, use the arrow keys to select the type of search you want to do. As you move the arrow keys to select your search, the Example section will change to illustrate a Topic search or a Keyword search. We will start with a Keyword search this time.

Dates covered by CD-ROM

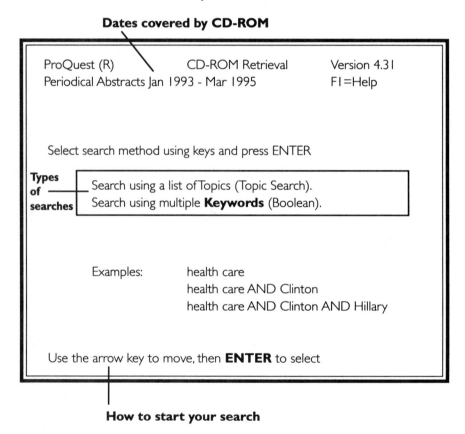

ProQuest (R)   CD-ROM Retrieval   Version 4.31
Periodical Abstracts Jan 1993 - Mar 1995   F1=Help

Select search method using keys and press ENTER

Types of searches
Search using a list of Topics (Topic Search).
Search using multiple **Keywords** (Boolean).

Examples: health care
                   health care AND Clinton
                   health care AND Clinton AND Hillary

Use the arrow key to move, then **ENTER** to select

How to start your search

At the next screen type in your keywords, then press the ENTER key to begin your search. When the computer is finished searching, the results of the search will show up at the bottom of the screen. Press the ENTER key to view the titles or press the F7 key to go directly to the citation and the abstract.

How to get help

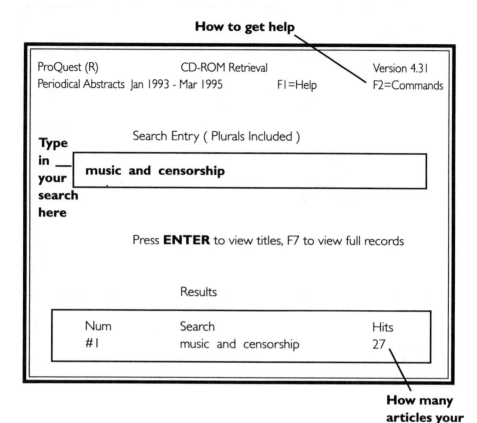

ProQuest (R)   CD-ROM Retrieval   Version 4.31
Periodical Abstracts Jan 1993 - Mar 1995   F1=Help   F2=Commands

Type in — your search here

Search Entry (Plurals Included)

music and censorship

Press **ENTER** to view titles, F7 to view full records

Results

Num	Search	Hits
#1	music and censorship	27

How many articles your search found

When you press the ENTER key a list of citations, with the most recent information first, comes up. Use the arrow keys or the Page Up/Page Down keys to navigate through this list.

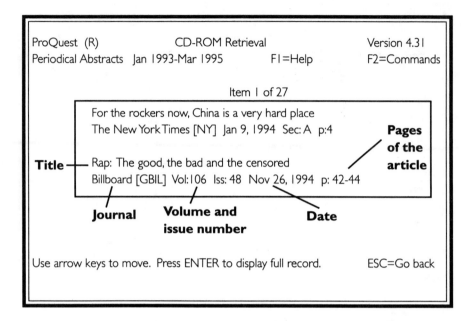

Highlight a record, then press the ENTER key to bring up the full record with the citation and abstract.

```
ProQuest (R)                    CD-ROM Retrieval                   Version 4.31
Periodical Abstracts  Jan 1993-Mar 1995      F1=Help             F2=Commands

                               Item 3 of 27
              Access No:  02163272
              Title:         Rap: The good, the bad and the censored
              Authors:     Benesch, Connie
              Journal:      Billboard [GBLL]  ISSN: 0006-2510  Jrnl Group: Business
Different                    Vol: 106   Iss: 48   Date:  Nov 26, 1994   p: 42-44
topics                       Type: Feature   Length: Medium   Illus: Photograph
you can      Subjects:    Rap music; Musical recordings; Musicians & conductors;
search                      Censorship; Radio programming; Television


              Abstract:  For male rappers, the original versions of their songs must be
                         cleaned up so they can be aired on radio or shown on TV.
                         Artists who have had their songs released in two forms and
                         the censoship of rap music in broadcasing are discussed.


    Use arrow keys or PgUp/PgDn to move.
                              + Next item. -Previous item.  ESC=Go back
```

To go to the next article

To navigate through the full records, use the arrow keys and the Page Up/Page Down keys as you would in the previous screens. The title, author, and journal name are well marked; don't forget to look at the subjects to find different terms or ideas for you to search. To print the full record, press the F2 key to bring up the correct commands.

A Topic search is very similar to a Subject Guide search in *Expanded Academic Index.* Highlight the Topic search line, then press the ENTER key.

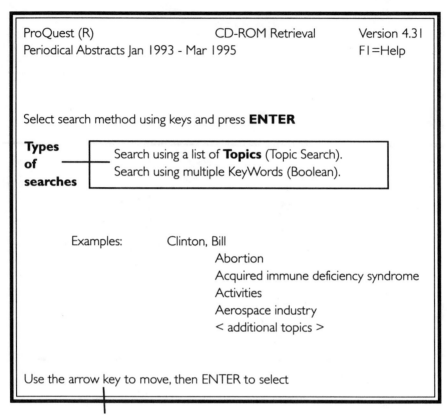

ProQuest (R)   CD-ROM Retrieval   Version 4.31
Periodical Abstracts Jan 1993 - Mar 1995   F1=Help

Select search method using keys and press **ENTER**

**Types
of
searches**   Search using a list of **Topics** (Topic Search).
                    Search using multiple KeyWords (Boolean).

          Examples: Clinton, Bill
                             Abortion
                             Acquired immune deficiency syndrome
                             Activities
                             Aerospace industry
                             < additional topics >

Use the arrow key to move, then ENTER to select

How to start your search

Now type in your search term. If your term is not there, check the list
of subjects to see if there is one close to yours or if you spelled your term
correctly. Use the arrow keys or the Page Up/Page Down keys to navigate
through the Topics.

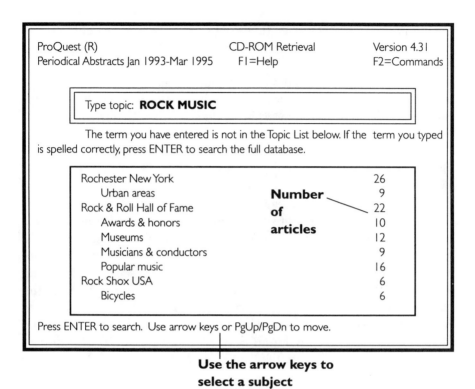

ProQuest (R)   CD-ROM Retrieval   Version 4.31
Periodical Abstracts Jan 1993-Mar 1995   F1=Help   F2=Commands

Type topic: **ROCK MUSIC**

The term you have entered is not in the Topic List below. If the term you typed
is spelled correctly, press ENTER to search the full database.

Rochester New York	26
Urban areas	9
Rock & Roll Hall of Fame	22
Awards & honors	10
Museums	12
Musicians & conductors	9
Popular music	16
Rock Shox USA	6
Bicycles	6

Number of articles

Press ENTER to search. Use arrow keys or PgUp/PgDn to move.

**Use the arrow keys to
select a subject**

Highlight a Topic, then press the ENTER key to bring up the citations found under that Topic. Continue as if performing a Keyword search.

Subject Specific Indexes

The general rule of thumb is that if colleges offer a major in a subject, an index exists covering the topic. Just as with the general subject indexes, there are a number of subject-specific indexes by different publishers. A few are listed in the previous *Readers' Guide to Periodical Literature* section. If you can search *Readers' Guide to Periodical Literature,* you should be able to search *Business Periodicals Index, Education Index, General Science Index,* and *Applied Science and Technology Index.*

But there are more indexes than just these. And they tend to be a bit more complicated. Searching options may not always be apparent on the screen, so it may take you longer to figure out how these indexes work. These tools also generally use a *controlled vocabulary.* This means that although searches will look like keyword searches, if you don't use the correct term that the specific index uses, you won't find all the information on that topic. A good example is the *ERIC Index. ERIC* is an education index, and if you searched on the word *teenagers* you would find 290 articles. That's not too bad a number, but if you searched on the word *adolescents,* you would find 8,505 articles!

To know which terms to use in a subject-specific index, check to see if it has a thesaurus. A thesaurus will list all the words the index uses for subjects. It will also tell you other subjects to use if your subject isn't there.

Subject-specific indexes on CD-ROM index scholarly or professional journals. For a freshman English composition paper this may be too advanced, so check with your instructor on what type of journals you should use for research. If your instructor would like to see citations from one or two scholarly journals, begin your search using a general subject index, then use the subject-specific index to find your last few citations.

Many libraries try to buy CD-ROMs from the same publisher (and thus are searched in the same way) to help students search quickly and effectively. But not all indexes are available from all publishers, so the chances are you will have to use more than one type of searching while you do your research. Here is a list of the most popular subject-specific indexes. These are mostly found at college and university libraries, so your school or public library may not have them.

ABI Inform (business; a ProQuest product)
American History and Life (history)
Business Periodicals Index (a Wilson product)
ComputerSelect (computer science)
Engineering Index (engineering)
General Science Index (a Wilson product)
Historical Abstracts (history)
Medline (medicine and health)
PsychLit (psychology)
Sociofile (sociology)

Using a CD-ROM index can dramatically reduce the time you spend researching a subject. But the first time you search an index on CD-ROM make sure you have plenty of time to figure out how the index works and if the library actually has the best index for you to use. The best place to start your research on CD-ROM is with a librarian.

Zak and Kristen would find many helpful articles, possibly *too* many, using any of the CD-ROM indexes. Before he uses the journal indexes, Zak could begin his research by using an encyclopedia article to learn about the history of capital punishment. Then he could use the *Statistical Abstract of the U.S.* to see how many people have been executed, for what crimes, over a specific period of time. But the *Statistical Abstract of the U.S.* does not have a heading for *capital punishment,* so Zak would have to look under *executions* to find the statistic he needs.

An encyclopedia or dictionary probably wouldn't help Kristen with her research paper. But, like Zak, she can use the *Statistical Abstract of the U.S.* Kristen could see how many hours a day children watch TV. Then she could compare that statistic to the amount of violent crimes committed over the same period of time. Both Kristen and Zak would have journal articles from the CD-ROM indexes and statistics to support their research papers.

Chapter 4

Secondary Research Using Online Services

Mark Vecchio and Carol Felstein

Not so very long ago, students working on term papers had little choice but to sit for hours in a library surrounded by piles of open books with little slips of scrap paper stuck haphazardly between pages. There's still no replacement for a large, well-stocked library for the purposes of research, especially if your subject requires you to peruse newspaper articles from, say, the mid-1860s. But for many research topics, there is a new and growing information resource that is accessible from any room in your house where there is a computer with a modem, and getting to this new resource is called *going online*.

When you do research online, the computing and memory capacities of your computer are connected by telephone to an electronic database, which is a collection of information arranged for ready analysis and retrieval. This is accomplished through a special telephone for computers, known as a modem. A few mouse clicks on your computer's monitor, and entire reference libraries are at your disposal.

The simplest way to go online is to join an online service. This chapter will describe the research tools available on the three most popular commercial online services, Prodigy, America Online, and CompuServe, as well as briefly discuss several of the largest specialized online databases.

WHAT YOU NEED TO GO ONLINE

A prerequisite to going online is having a computer equipped with a modem. Nowadays modems come in a variety of shapes, sizes, and prices, but the most important consideration in getting a modem (besides cost) is speed. As of 1995, the best (i.e., the fastest) mass market modems transmit information back and forth through your telephone line at the rate of 28,800 baud, or bps (bits per second)—when shopping, you can simply call it "28.8." If you're buying a modem and you can afford a 28.8 model, get one. A fast modem will enable you to request information with one click of your mouse, look down at your watch to see how many hours you have left before your term paper is due in class the next morning, and look back up to see the information you asked for. At the opposite end of the spectrum are modems that run at 2,400 baud. With a "2400" modem, you click your mouse to request information, go to the kitchen to make a pot of coffee, and return just in time to see your request scroll languorously onto the screen. As of the writing of this book, a happy medium of cost and speed is a 14.4 modem.

The second major consideration is the type of computer you have and the operating system you use. This chapter will assume that you have either a PC running Windows or DOS, or a Macintosh.

To join an online service, just call the service's toll-free number and request a membership kit (Prodigy, 800-776-3449; America Online, 800-827-6364; CompuServe, 800-862-1272). The service will send you a disk (be sure to specify what operating system you have) and sign-up instructions.

Choosing an Online Service

Choosing between Prodigy, AOL (short for America Online), and CompuServe (or CIS, an acronym for CompuServe Information Service) is a matter of your needs and your taste. As you will see later in this chapter, CompuServe has, by comparison with the other two, vast resources for research; it can also be vastly more expensive if you actually use those resources. It is recommended that you browse each service, something that is easy and cheap to do, since all three offer one free trial month.

A fourth mass market online service, the Microsoft Network, expected to have features similar to the others, is being introduced as a component of the newest version (as of this writing) of the Windows operating system, Windows 95. The software for the new service is bundled in the

Windows 95 package, and the click of an icon will allow new customers to try it out. This may increase competition among all the online services, and perhaps, for a while at least, the public will pay somewhat less for more service as a result.

Access to a standard array of subjects is essentially the same in Prodigy, America Online, and CompuServe. When you sign on, opening screens provide labels or icons for broad categories, such as News, Entertainment, Children, Reference, Computers, Health, and so on. Click on any one of these and a subcategory of choices comes up on the screen. Or take a short cut, using the equivalent of a computer *go to* command. In Prodigy it is "Jump ____," in AOL, "Keyword ____," and in CompuServe, "Go ____." Fill in the blank with the subject you wish to pursue; e.g., "Jump <u>Homework Helper</u>"; "Keyword <u>Reference</u>"; "Go <u>Encyclopedia</u>."

Costs.   The following cost information for the three online services was valid as of October 1995. Even when dollar amounts change, however, the pricing structure of each service usually remains the same. All three services charge $9.95 per month for up to five hours of online usage; introductory packages for the first month usually offer about ten hours free—special packages may vary.

CompuServe charges by service categories: most things are included in the basic monthly fee with an additional surcharge for some "premium services." Over 3,000 products and services (e.g., news, weather, entertainment, etc.) are available to members for up to five hours a month with an additional hourly charge for extra time. Premium services (e.g., many of the online databases, unfortunately) all carry surcharges that vary from service to service—rates are available online.

Prodigy has a similar structure, with basic "core" services and so-called "plus" services, but its standard price scheme does not differentiate between the two; other plans (more hours for more money) do. It also offers premium services, at additional hourly or monthly rates.

America Online has the simplest pricing plan, one of its attractions. You pay a flat fee for five hours of use and a nominal hourly rate for every hour after the initial five: this includes every service you can find on AOL, except a handful of special services such as sending paper ("snail") mail or faxes through AOL.

PRODIGY

Prodigy has nearly two million subscribers (*New York Times* Business Section, June 28, 1995), and is designed for mass appeal. Prodigy is a relative lightweight in terms of reference resources offered as part of its own service, compared to America Online and CompuServe. (A major exception to this is Homework Helper, an electronic library offered through Prodigy, which permits extensive research; see below.) It is possible to get satisfying results for certain types of research using Prodigy, particularly for assignments dealing with current events or government, or for those few assignments that can be adequately met with the use of a good general encyclopedia.

As soon as you connect to Prodigy, if you have not chosen a special JUMPWORD (the Prodigy term for the keywords you enter to get where you want to go in the service), you will see a highlight screen. The screen features news articles you can select on the left side, and a menu bar on the right side. Most of Prodigy's feature articles on these introductory screens include a few advertisements, and the bottom third of just about every screen invites you to join CD music clubs, buy cars, read about stocks (for a fee, of course), download software, and so on.

Reference Choices

Reference choices include: Encyclopedia, Political Profile, White House Memo, Software Guide, Homework Helper, and Newsstand. Each of these can be accessed by typing "Jump..." and filling in your choice as named here. Prodigy used to have a main reference screen, but for some reason has dropped it, while still keeping the same reference resources.

Encyclopedia.   A good general encyclopedia often serves as a starting point for a research project. Prodigy offers Grolier's *Academic American Encyclopedia,* with 33,000 articles in 10 million words. Quarterly updates keep the information current. Zak could read about capital punishment throughout Western history, print the article to paper or disk, and extract whatever facts he needed.

To get there, type "Jump *encyclopedia*", then fill in part or all of the subject name. The screen comes up with an index of articles starting with the letters you typed; tab to or click on the appropriate article, and it will come up on the next screen. You can take notes, print the entire article, or download it to your computer's hard drive or a floppy disk. Cross-references are provided at the end of each article, and can be brought up on your screen by clicking on them, or by highlighting them and pressing ENTER.

Current events offered in news stories on Prodigy are tied in to the encyclopedia. Type "Jump *Background*" when reading a news article to get appropriate reference articles to choose from.

Political Profile.   Prodigy offers good material for political science or government research. Political Profile has biographies of each member of the current Congress. It tells you how your representatives voted on key issues, and what special interest groups (often known as ·PACs or Political Action Committees) contributed money to each representative's election campaign. It compares votes cast and contributions received by members of Congress.

A number of organizations, such as the American Civil Liberties Union, rate congressional representatives. Prodigy offers those ratings.

Congressional committees are described and members listed. Profiles of each state's representation and committee membership are available.

Write to Washington.   E-mail addresses are provided for government officials, all the way up to the president, for congressional committees, and for FAQs (Frequently Asked Questions). You can search for an e-mail address by entering a last name, a state name, an organization name, or a FAQ. Kristen could e-mail her local congressional representatives and ask about their views on the effects of television violence on children, and how they plan to vote on recent measures to mandate chips in televisions that will permit parents to block out stations they do not believe to be suitable for their children to watch.

White House Memo.   Presidential and cabinet briefings, speeches, and transcripts can be brought up on your screen and printed if you wish. The most recent ones appear together, and past materials are grouped by subject.

News and Newsstand.   Current daily news is updated every few hours. A menu choice on the right for AP ONLINE offers access to hourly updates of Associated Press news releases. Prodigy is also the gateway to several daily newspapers' online editions. There is a fee for an Atlanta and a Los Angeles paper, but a Rhode Island service is free.

Select "Newsstand" from the news screen or type "Jump *Newsstand*". Menu choices on the next screen include: Access Atlanta, a newspaper;

American Heritage, a history magazine; Congressional Reports; Newsday
Direct, a newspaper; Newsweek Interactive, an electronic version of the
weekly news magazine; and Timeslink, a newspaper. Most of these resources are either charged to "plus" Prodigy time, or have their own additional monthly fees for joining, which you do the first time you select
any one of them.

Access Atlanta leads you to a daily newspaper, the *Atlanta Journal
Constitution Online*. It is a fee service and requires a first-time use enrollment.

American Heritage magazine has articles and color photos of topics
relevant to American history, politics, culture, biography, etc. For example,
the May/June 1995 issue focused on World War II. There is an "Archives"
section, but only for a few recent issues.

With Newsday Direct, you can access current issues of this Long Island newspaper. Most useful for reference is the "Archive Retrieval" menu,
which references articles dating back a few years. Select Newsday Archive
Retrieval, then type a keyword—i.e., a word or phrase that embodies
what you wish to search. Next, select dates to search between. Choose
which sections your search should focus on: news, business, viewpoints,
etc.

Newsweek Interactive lets you access the national news magazine and
offers articles from current and recent issues, illustrated with color photographs. Unless your computer is of very recent, high-speed, high-
memory vintage, the time it takes for the pictures to come up on your
screen is not worth it: even on a 486-DX2/66 computer with a 14.4 modem, it is annoyingly slow.

With Timeslink, the *Los Angeles Times* is online for a fee of $4.95
month. Current articles are as useful as in any other of the online news
services; the Associated Press is likely to be the best. But if you decide to
do a term paper or doctoral thesis on the Academy Awards, this is the
place to look. Archives back to 1992 may be helpful for general topics.

Homework Helper

Homework Helper is a service to which Prodigy serves as a gateway. It
requires separate enrollment and a basic monthly fee ($9.95 at the time
this is being written) plus an additional fee for extra time. An alternative
plan is a flat $6 an hour, and no monthly fee. Homework Helper is an
electronic library of over 700,000 articles from newspapers, magazines,
and books, as well as numerous maps and photographs. The articles are
updated daily. They are accessed by keyword searching: you type in one

or more words (typically a subject, author, or other identifying phrase), and Homework Helper's search engine scans *all* of its stored texts for those words. The results of the search will be all of the articles in Homework Helper's database that contain instances of your search words. You may use Boolean logic ("and," "or," and "not" to narrow or widen your search results) in your searches.

For a successful search, the screen comes up with a list of articles by title, author, and size (in megabytes). Highlight a title that looks like a source of potential interest, and click the Download button, or just double-click the article title. The text of the article is transferred to your computer screen. Browse it quickly, and if it appears to be what you need, click on the Save button on the menu bar across the top. You are asked for a path and file name; the text is downloaded in a matter of seconds (assuming you're using something faster than a 2400 modem). After you finish downloading articles (you can also highlight selections within articles to download), sign off Homework Helper, open your word processing program, and open the files, which you can then review and print at your leisure. It is all there for you, including the citation, which ends each article.

This service has an exhaustive amount of material on all sorts of topics at moderate cost. Note that professional scholarly journals are not heavily represented; daily newspapers and mass-market periodicals are. It is recommended that you have a fair idea of what you're looking for before you start browsing through Homework Helper: the sheer volume of offerings can be off-putting. But this is a valuable new research tool with very user-friendly access.

AMERICA ONLINE

For the past few years, America Online has been the fastest growing commercial online service (in 1994 it *tripled* its subscriptions, and by mid-1995 had more than three million subscribers), in part because of its attractive, easy to use graphical interface, and in part because of its simple, affordable pricing. Perhaps another reason is that on AOL alone of the three major services, your online identity is a name of your choosing rather than a seemingly random numeric or alphanumeric string. One qualification, though: any name that someone else is as likely to think up as you are is probably already taken; so if your name is John or Jane Smith, or if you want to be known as "Batman" or "Cat Woman," you will be faced with a creative challenge.

A note about AOL's pleasant graphical interface: you will pay a price for it—in wait-time. Whenever you enter an area on AOL for the first time (or a period of time has passed since you last entered the area), a message box will appear on your screen that says, "Please wait while we add new art to America Online," and a series of graphical images will be invisibly transmitted to your computer. While this is happening, your system will be totally occupied; you sit and wait. The good news is that if you have a reasonably fast computer and modem (i.e., at least a 486 PC with a 14.4 modem), these updates shouldn't take more than between five and twenty seconds each. However, if you have an old clunker with a 2400 modem…time for lunch.

Getting Around

When you first sign onto America Online, you are presented with a marbled white window. To the left is a large button that tells you if you have any incoming e-mail waiting to be read; to the right are a few icons that, when clicked, lead to some activity or news item or vendor being featured at that particular hour.

Clicking on the thin box at the bottom of the window that reads MAIN MENU will take you to another window with a series of rectangular buttons that all lead to AOL's major areas of interest. These include the Newsstand, the Internet Connection, Education, a Reference Desk, and so on. In these general areas of interest you will be presented with icons and listboxes that you can click on to get to specific *forums*.

Forums are individual services within the larger community of America Online—for example, the Online Campus, which offers full electronic courses in most liberal arts subjects, holds academic contests, and so on.

The easiest way to navigate through AOL is to use the KEYWORD facility. To do this, either select "Keyword…" from the *Go To* menu, or press CTRL-K for Windows, or Open-Apple-K for Macs, and a window will appear asking you for your keyword(s). Type the words you know will take you where you want to go, and voila! there you'll be. If you can't remember a keyword, use common sense to make a guess, and if the area exists you should get there; for example, using KEYWORD *dictionary*, or *webster*, or *merriam-webster* (with or without a hyphen) will all get you to the Merriam-Webster Dictionary. The KEYWORD facility is not case sensitive, so don't worry about capitalization.

General Features

Software and Resource Libraries. AOL, like its competitors, is bursting at the seams with downloadable software. In addition, AOL has a variety of "libraries" with such things as articles on the general relativity theory and a complete and fully searchable text of *The Federalist Papers*. Most of the individual services on AOL offer their own libraries of downloadable software and resources: look for icons labeled such, or sometimes labeled "archives" or the like.

You can browse AOL's general software library for educational resources by going to the Software Center (KEYWORD *software*). Once there, click on Search the Libraries, and a search window will come up. Click the check box next to Education, and type in a subject category: e.g., "history," or "science." If you're too specific, you won't get anything (for instance, don't type in "Cuban Missile Crisis" and get your hopes up).

Message Boards. Message Boards are exactly what they sound like. You select a topic from a list, and what you get is a collection of messages that have been posted by other AOL members on that topic. The messages are in ascending date order. You can respond to any message by posting your own, which gets added to the bottom of the list. When you read and respond to a Message Board, you are alone, that is, there is no real-time interactivity (compare this with Chat Rooms, below).

Message Boards can be useful for research when the topic matches the one you're working on. In that case you have a tailor-made forum in which you can test your ideas and get feedback from other, necessarily interested (or else they wouldn't be reading your messages), people.

Chat Rooms. "Rooms" are interactive windows shared by any number of AOL subscribers simultaneously, who can "chat" with each other. To chat with the other people in a room, type your message on the bottom of the window and "send" it by clicking on the Send button or by pressing the ENTER key; when you do that, your message is posted in the main part of the window for all people in the room to read.

There are "live" discussions on a wide variety of subjects all the time in rooms on AOL. Check forums associated with topics you're interested in for such discussions.

Performing Searches. Several of AOL's centers, such as *Scientific American* Online, have a database of articles and abstracts that can be viewed, saved to disk, and/or printed. Finding such material is a matter of performing a simple search using keywords. Just as it sounds, this process is almost identical to that of using KEYWORDS to hop from service to service: when you're presented with a Search window, you type in words associated with what you are looking for, and press the ENTER key (or click on the button that says LIST ARTICLES or something similar). You can use Boolean expressions to narrow your search parameters.

Some tips on performing searches are to try being a little general at first, and see what response you get; if 200 articles come up, try again, this time being more specific (except: see "Hints for Searching *Compton's Online Encyclopedia*," below). Also, try more than one way to find something; if you're looking for information on gorillas, try searching on "primates" and "Jane Goodall" as well.

America Online's Internet Connection *and* WebCrawler

AOL offers Internet access right on its Main Menu screen: just click on "Internet Connection" (KEYWORD *Internet*) and you will be presented with a window of options allowing you access to Internet newsgroups, FTP, gopher, and WAIS, as well as AOL's "WebCrawler" (KEYWORD *WebCrawler*), which is its engine for searching the World Wide Web. See Chapter 5, "Secondary Research Using the Internet," for details on how to use Internet services.

Educational Resources on America Online

America Online, to the benefit of students (and teachers, by the way), has targeted education as one of its service priorities. Its educational forums range from help with study skills (KEYWORD *study*), to eight-week online courses in most subjects (KEYWORD *classes*); from exam preparation (KEYWORD *exam prep*), to Student Access Online (KEYWORD *student access*), which offers the extremely helpful student support services of the Princeton Review. To browse these forums, click on Education on the Main Menu.

One of AOL's most useful educational resources is the Academic Assistance Center (KEYWORD *AAC*). Once there, click on "Academic Assistance Classrooms," then choose either "Humanities" or "Math and Science," and you will find yourself in a room in which you can ask a teacher questions and get help right then and there (the AAC's schedule permitting—click on "Weekly Schedule" for information). If you don't get what you need there, try the "Teacher Pager": type out your question and send it, and usually within the same day (the next day at the latest) you'll get an e-mail response from a teacher.

General Reference Resources

Compton's Online Encyclopedia.   America Online provides access to *Compton's Online Encyclopedia* (KEYWORD *encyclopedia*). The file contains eight million words, 5,200 full-length articles, 26,023 capsule articles, and 63,503 index entries as of mid-1995, and is updated frequently.

There are two ways to search the encyclopedia: by titles of articles or by full text. Searching by title will get you articles in the encyclopedia whose titles contain the words you used in your search; e.g., if you search by title using the words "women's suffrage," the search engine would locate and list all article titles with those words in them.

Searching on full text will get you a list of all entries that contain the words you searched on *anywhere in the text of the article*, and not necessarily adjacent to each other. So performing a full-text search for "women's suffrage" would get you a long list of entries that had these two words *somewhere* within them, including articles that mentioned "women's" in one place and "suffrage" in another, perhaps in a totally different context. If you perform your search this way, you'll probably want to make your keywords more specific; e.g., "women's suffrage England teetotaler."

General tips for choosing search words include:

1.   Avoid abbreviations: e.g., type "European Economic Community" rather than "EEC."
2.   Avoid slang and nicknames: e.g., type "Elizabeth I" rather than "the virgin queen."
3.   Avoid being overly specific: e.g., type "bow" rather than "violin bow."
4.   If you find no matches, try using a synonym: e.g., change "farming" to "agriculture."
5.   To narrow a search, include additional words: e.g., change "physics" to "particle physics."

Merriam-Webster Dictionary.   The *Merriam-Webster Online Dictionary* (KEYWORD *dictionary,* or *Webster,* or *Merriam-Webster*—not case or hyphen sensitive; that is, it doesn't matter if you use upper- or lowercase letters or include or omit the hyphen) will give you the spelling, pronunciation, and part(s) of speech of any word in American English, as well as brief etymologies and Webster's patented terse definitions.

To search for a word in the dictionary, simply type the word in the

---

Hints for Searching *Compton's Online Encyclopedia*

1. Search words must be at least three letters long.
2. Wildcard characters can be used for spelling variations and broader searches, as follows:

    * — Stands in for any combination of characters; e.g., "bon*" will call up listings on Napoleon *Bonaparte*, *bonsai* trees, and the *bongo* variety of antelope, among other things.

    ? — Stands in for a single character; e.g., "bon?" will limit the results of your search to *bond*, *bone*, and the city *Bonn* in Germany.
3. *Spaces* in a search phrase operate exactly like the word *and*; e.g., "women's suffrage England teetotaler" is treated in exactly the same way by the search engine as if you had typed "women's and suffrage and England and teetotaler." Ditto for "capital punishment United States."
4. Use *Boolean expressions* ("and," "or," and "not") to narrow your search.

---

upper-right box and press the ENTER key. If you're not sure of the spelling, type in your best guess for the first three letters, followed by an asterisk (°), then press ENTER.

You have the option of searching either for a word and its definition alone or for how a particular word is used all through the entire dictionary. To do the former, click on Single Word and type in your word. To search for a word's usage throughout the dictionary, click on Full Text and type in your word: a list of words will appear that all use the word you started with in one way or another. Click on any word in the list to see its definition.

Also of interest is the Merriam-Webster Word Exchange, which is a series of message boards devoted to discussing and resolving questions about words, usage, grammar, etc.

College Online. This forum (KEYWORD *College Online*) has a listbox of subject headings (e.g., "Communications," "Psychology," etc.). Click on one of these headings, then in the next window select "AOL/Internet Resources": you'll get a description of what resources are available for that subject on America Online as well as what's available just through AOL's Internet gateway.

Mini-Lesson Libraries. Mini-lessons are downloadable text files containing teachers' answers to previously asked questions in the Academic

Assistance Classrooms and on the Teacher Pager (see "Educational Resources on America Online" above). Go to the Academic Assistance Center (KEYWORD *AAC*), then select "Mini-Lesson Libraries" and choose your preferred subject.

Library of Congress Online.   Don't get your hopes up—this isn't the entire catalog of one of the world's best-stocked libraries available for selection and download. The Library of Congress Online (KEYWORD *LOC*) is a collection of rotating exhibits, each of which has its own set of downloadable "artifacts." For example, one exhibit is from the Vatican Library, which displayed such artifacts as a letter from Henry VIII to Anne Boleyn and drawings of sunspots by Galileo. Extremely interesting stuff, especially if you're looking for something to base a paper on. Other exhibits include the Dead Sea Scrolls, "1492: An Ongoing Voyage," the Renaissance Information Center, and others. New exhibits are added regularly.

In addition, the Library of Congress Online has message boards, e-mail directories of scholars, and chat rooms.

Literature

Barron's Booknotes.   These are the same as Monarch and Cliff's Notes: commentaries on classic works of literature. The database (KEYWORD *Barrons*) is searchable by author, title, and keyword(s), so it is possible to pull up articles by theme. Articles include: excerpts of classic literary criticism (e.g., Melville on Hawthorne), author biographies, plot and character analyses, and discussions of the literary merit of particular works.

Electronic Books.   Tired of reading printed pages? Miss your chance to bombard yourself with electrons today? Do your eyes feel like they need a *real* challenge?

Then E-Text is for you! (KEYWORD *etext*). Click on "Palmtop Paperbacks," and choose from dozens of downloadable electronic books. All you need to view and/or print them is a text editor or word processing program.

Bible.   AOL has a searchable full text of the Old and New Testaments online (KEYWORD *Bible*).

Science Resources

Scientific American Online.   Recent issues of *Scientific American* (KEY-WORD *scientific*) can be read, downloaded, and printed, as well as searched for every occurrence of a given word or phrase. Back issues to May 1994 can be also searched by keyword (select "Search Back Issues"). Abstracts of 4,338 feature articles dating back to May 1948 can also be searched by keyword, a valuable feature: just double-click on "Search Annual Indexes."

National Academy of Science (NAS) Online.   NAS Online (KEYWORD *NAS*) gives you access to the National Academy of Science database of news articles summarizing the institution's major reports. "Sound Off on Science" features opinion pieces by experts from government, industry, and the academic world. The "Bookstore" is a catalog of nearly 900 titles from the National Academy Press. The "Lecture Room" is a chat center for science topics. "NAS Archives" offers text and graphics files for downloading.

National Geographic Society Online.   The National Geographic Society forum (KEYWORD *NGS*) offers downloadable maps (click on "NGS Online Atlas"—these maps, unfortunately, cannot be viewed online), articles both for viewing and for downloading, message boards, and "Ask Geographic," a facility for posting a question directly to the Society. You can also order back issues dating as far back as December 1914.

Network Earth Online.   The Network Earth Resource Library (KEY-WORD *Network Earth*) offers information on the environment and the movement to protect the environment. It has press releases from environmental organizations and government agencies, an index of the major environmental organizations, book reviews from the American Library Association, reports about major environmental issues, and updates of congressional activity on environmental issues, including the environmental voting records of members of Congress. All this is full-text searchable through the search utility on Network Earth's main screen, which responds to keywords with articles, book abstracts with bibliographic citations, and transcripts of Network Earth shows.

Terms of Environment.   Available resources include the Federal Environmental Protection Agency's (EPA) online dictionary. It defines the more commonly used environmental terms appearing in EPA publications, news releases, and other agency documents available to the public.

Other Science Resources.   Other science resources available through America Online include:

- Access Excellence (KEYWORD *excellence*): This service is largely oriented towards assisting teachers. It has articles on biology and biotechnology.
- Better Health and Medical Forum (KEYWORD *health*): The Better Health and Medical Forum has a Home Medical Guide, and other information on health issues.
- Microsoft Knowledge Base (KEYWORD *knowledge base*): This is a searchable library on computer use and technology, with over 18,000 articles on Microsoft products.
- Computer Terms Dictionary (KEYWORD *computer terms*): This dictionary is just what it sounds like; keyword searchable.

Government Resources

The Washington Week in Review.   This service (KEYWORD WWIR) is a twin in content to Prodigy's "Congressional Report," whose feature is here called "Capital Facts." You can find information on federal agencies, Congress and its committees, the past year's elections, and the Supreme Court. Also available are some of the keystone documents of American history, such as the Mayflower Compact and Patrick Henry's "give me liberty or give me death" speech.

The White House Forum.   Similar to Prodigy's "White House Memo," the White House Forum (KEYWORD *White House*) has press releases on government topics from the budget to environment to labor. You can also e-mail the president here.

Congressional Quarterly Online.   This service (KEYWORD *CQ*) reports on current federal government events.

News Resources

America Online has current news, updated every few hours, and also offers the day's *New York Times* and the week's *Time* magazine. These texts are not keyword searchable, although the current day's news is (KEYWORD *US News*). AOL offers news, grouped by geographic areas, in much greater detail than does Prodigy. For example, you can check on news from the Pacific Rim, Sub-Sahara, and other regions.

The Newsstand: Online Newspapers and Magazines. AOL's Newsstand is just that—the electronic equivalent of a well-supplied newsstand in an upscale hotel lobby. For newspapers, it offers @times (the *New York Times*), the *Orlando Sentinel,* the *San Jose Mercury News, Time* magazine, and a host of other current periodicals covering a wide variety of special interests to be perused when any amount of research is just too much to contemplate: computers, travel, audio equipment, home, finance, business, etc.

Time magazine has keyword-searchable archives dating back to August 1993. Current and recent issues can be read online. Zak could search "capital punishment" for the past few years of relevant articles.

@times, an electronic version of the *New York Times,* is not searchable. It offers "The Times Looks Back," with selected feature articles. Here you can do your Academy Awards research paper—the ceremonies are covered in detail over many years. Need to do research on the 1969 Woodstock Festival, or the fall of Saigon in April 1975, or the 1963 March on Washington? They are all here, but there isn't much else. This feature is fun, but is limited to a few major pop culture milestones.

The current day's *Chicago Tribune* is online, with searchable archives.

The electronic edition of the *San Jose Mercury News,* the Mercury Center, is archived and searchable back to 1993; but the most important feature here is that this is a gateway into the "Newspaper Library" (KEYWORD *MC Library*), one of AOL's rare premium services, costing (as of this writing) 15¢ per minute between the hours of 6 P.M. and 6 A.M. weekdays, and 80¢ per minute between 6 A.M. and 6 P.M. weekdays, plus regular AOL connect-time charges. The Newspaper Library has the electronic archives of eighteen newspapers across the country back to the 1980s (the specific year varies by paper), all of which are keyword searchable, with downloadable articles.

"Newshound" is a new electronic "clippings" service offered by the Mercury Center. It searches articles and classified ads from the *San Jose Mercury News,* the *New York Times,* and several news wire services to match your custom request, then sends the "clippings" to your e-mail address. If Kristen belonged to this service, she could receive articles on current initiatives regarding television violence and the impact on children.

News Forums. C-SPAN Online is a downloadable library of text files: bills from the House of Representatives, C-SPAN program transcripts, reports, and articles. C-SPAN's Political Resource Center is much like

Prodigy's Congressional Report. It has a chat room, a message board, summaries of current House bills, a congressional calendar, roll calls, and voting records. It lists the members and committees in both houses of Congress, as well as reports on PAC (Political Action Committee) affiliations for presidential candidates, and congressional candidates by state.

The ABC News Library offers archives of transcripts from news and commentary shows, including ABC News election polling results, and software libraries of graphic image files. Also available are maps of regions, countries, and cities worldwide stored as downloadable files, and other news-related graphics.

The CNN Newsroom Guide has articles dating back to the early 1990s, downloadable maps, and a message board about current events.

COMPUSERVE

CompuServe (CIS—for CompuServe Information Service) is the oldest of the three major commercial online services, and hence the most far-reaching—by a wide margin—with respect to affiliated and subsidiary databases. In fact, to review all the research resources available on CIS would take an entire book at least as large—and probably larger—than this one. For this reason, this section will attempt to point you in the right direction to do research on CompuServe, a reference providing you with leads to major resources with their respective GO-words (similar to Prodigy's JUMP and AOL's KEYWORD functions).

It is possible to connect to CompuServe with just a generic communications software program, which will limit you to a menu-and-command line interface. It is strongly recommended that you use CompuServe's CIM (CompuServe Information Manager) software, which can be downloaded from the service or sent by mail (see "What You Need to Go Online" above for CompuServe's toll-free number).

Getting Around

When you sign onto CompuServe you will be presented with an icon-filled SERVICES window, somewhat similar in appearance and operation to AOL's Main Menu: clicking on the icons, labeled variously "News," "Magazines," "Reference," "Education," "Internet," etc., will take you to the major areas of interest within CIS. Beyond this screen, icons are relatively scarce compared to America Online: click on "Reference," for example, and you will be presented with a listbox of reference services;

click on the name of the reference you want to access and you will get another listbox of options.

As with Prodigy and America Online, the fastest way to move between services on CompuServe is to use the GO utility. You invoke this either by clicking on the green traffic light icon near the top of the screen, or by pressing CTRL-G, then typing the GO-word of the service you're looking for. Unlike with AOL, however, if you don't know the GO-word of the service you want, common sense will get you only so far. Although several services within CompuServe have obvious labels (e.g., GO *encyclopedia* for *Grolier's Encyclopedia,* and GO *dictionary* for the *American Heritage Dictionary*) others have labels consisting of abbreviations, truncations, and concatenations: GO *HLTDB* for Health Database Plus, GO *MagDB* for Magazine Database Plus, and GO *GloRep* for Global Report, for instance. Luckily you can get comprehensive lists to choose from by executing GO *quick,* which will enable you to hunt for services by category, or to get a list of every service available on CIS—which you'll need the better part of a day, perhaps two, to browse through.

General Features

As described above in the section on relative costs, CompuServe includes some "premium services," which carry surcharges *over and above* the normal connect-time charges. Thus, before accessing any database, look in the service's listbox for the words "Pricing Information." If you don't, you'll be in for quite a shock when, just after congratulating yourself on your first successful search, you read the words, "Total charges thus far: $9."

Forums and Software Libraries.   *Forums* on CompuServe are similar to chat rooms on America Online (they are *not* the same as forums on AOL: AOL forums are equivalent to CompuServe *services*—it can be confusing).

On CompuServe, in order to enter a forum you have to join it first. Upon entering a forum for the first time you will be prompted for your name and asked whether you want to join, visit or leave. Visiting may restrict you to certain areas within the forum. When you join, most forums require you to use your real name; some allow you to use a nickname.

Forums have message boards and conference rooms where members can participate in real-time discussions. CIS forums are also the source for CompuServe's extensive software libraries, which, like the ones on the other services, contain educational text files, graphics images, and programs available for download. For the purposes of research, these software libraries will be most forums' main attraction; the message boards tend to be more person-to-person-oriented than those on AOL, and there are few if any conference rooms on CIS devoted to providing online study assistance.

CompuServe's Internet Service and "NetLauncher"

Also on its main menu of Basic Services, CompuServe has an icon for Internet access (GO *Internet*), which, as of this writing, includes gateways to Usenet newsgroups, FTP, and telnet. In order to surf the Web, you will need to download (or order by phone) CIS's new *NetLauncher* software (GO *NetLauncher*), a three-in-one program built on the SPRY™ Mosaic™ browser, which gives full World Wide Web access. See Chapter Five, "Secondary Research Using the Internet," for details on how to use Internet services.

CompuServe's Databases

Overview. Because there are so many databases available on CIS, it is far beyond the scope of this book to discuss them individually. Instead, you will find here summary instructions for accessing information resources on CompuServe, followed by selected lists of the databases along with their GO-words.

The two main gateways to research tools on CompuServe are through the Reference and Education icons in the main SERVICE window. There are overlaps between these two gateways. Such diverse services as *Grolier's Academic American Encyclopedia, Dissertation Abstracts, Current Events, Books in Print,* and *Magill's Survey of Cinema* are available here.

Summary Instructions for Accessing CompuServe Databases. All reference sources on CompuServe, when clicked on, should come up with a window offering the following choices (as appropriate, depending on whether you've clicked on a premium service):

- "Description" leads to a concise description of what kind of resource(s) the service offers.
- "Search Guidelines" explains the ins and outs of performing successful searches. Each service has its own search guidelines, and even though these guidelines are often similar through several dif-

even though these guidelines are often similar through several different services, it is worthwhile to review them for each individual service, as variations can be significant.

- "Pricing Information" explicitly details all the costs of the service. (Often is it wise to look here first.)
- "Access ____" takes you to the service itself. If the service is a premium, this option will be followed by a dollar sign in parentheses: e.g., "Access Marquis Who's Who ($)." It is often possible to click on this option and do a little light reconnaissance, as the surcharges of premium services usually don't start adding up until you execute your first search. Thus, for instance, you can breeze through IQuest's menu structure (try not to get lost in it—it's huge), and not spend a red cent as long as you don't perform any searches.

Some services might have one or a few more options, such as "Sample Search Results," and so on. Learning how to access a database successfully is simply a matter of carefully reading all of its preliminary information.

Some Highlights of CompuServe's Database Library. Access to CompuServe includes *Grolier's Academic American Encyclopedia* (also on Prodigy) and the *American Heritage Dictionary* (also on AOL); CompuServe's other encyclopedia, the *Hutchinson,* has the added feature of graphics images that can be viewed and downloaded. The *Information Please Almanac* can be browsed either by keyword or by category. *MAGELLAN Maps* (we don't know why it's spelled in all caps) offers color continental maps that you can view on screen and save to disk. If you want a greater selection of maps, access *MAGELLAN Geographic Maps,* an extended service. And last, there is *HealthNet,* which has basic articles on symptoms, diseases, drugs, etc.

KNOWLEDGE INDEX (GO *KI*) is a collection of over 100 databases in twenty-six subject categories from agriculture to social sciences. You can invoke listings, both alphabetical and by subject, of KNOWLEDGE INDEX's available databases.

IQuest (GO *IQuest*) is a gateway to over 450 databases. It is menu-driven by subject, and has its own help files. For most liberal arts subjects, select "General Interest" from IQuest's Main Menu, and go from there. IQuest exacts a charge for performing searches, but other charges (e.g., for obtaining full-text articles, ordering reports, etc.) vary according to which database you access. As with other premium database services, you will always see a running total of charges at the bottom of the window. Should Zak or Kristen come into some extra money, their respective search needs for material on capital punishment or the effects of television violence on children could be met comprehensively here. Kristen, for example, could limit her search to psychological studies correlating violent acts by kids with their television viewing habits.

ONLINE DATABASES: DIALOG AND LEXIS/NEXIS

There are a number of general and specialized online databases used for reference by librarians and other professional researchers. The size and complexity of these databases renders them inappropriate for many student projects, but there may come a time or a special research assignment when this is the best way to go.

Many libraries, particularly the central branches of public libraries and college and university libraries, subscribe to online databases. A student with a research need that has not been satisfied in other formats can go to the reference librarian and request an online reference interview. The librarian sits down with the researcher to establish if the information desired should be in abstracts (summaries) or text, explains the charges for such a search, and usually has a form that the researcher must fill out. These search charges may range, on average, anywhere from $5 to $100 (*American Library Association Guide to Information Access*, edited by Sandy Whitely; Random House, 1994). Public libraries generally charge just what they must to recover their actual online costs for your search; they tend not to pass along overhead costs. Some libraries will also absorb these costs and not charge them back to you. Your librarian will explain the individual library's policy to you. College and university libraries may have special departments for online searches.

The three commercial services described above, especially Compu-Serve, also serve as gateways to various online databases. However the complexity and cost of online database services, and the sheer mass of material available, make it both impractical and expensive for the novice user to venture out on his or her own at this time. The recommended approach is to sit down with a reference librarian who will help frame and then conduct the search. The library charges are likely to be a great bargain compared to the individual cost. On the other hand, it has been said that knowledge is power, and for the ambitious searcher, these databases offer an amazing level of access to the world's stores of knowledge.

DIALOG

DIALOG, owned by Knight Ridder Information, Inc., is the major database provider, with over 600 databases covering literally a world of information (news reports, articles, abstracts, and citations in the hundreds of millions). It is the biggest (judged by actual number of files) and is very involved—it is not for beginners. DIALOG is a command-, not menu-driven system, and the user must enter specific codes (not impossible to master, if you elect to study them, but nothing you would figure out intuitively) to frame a search. It is better to let the librarian do it, unless your goal is to become an online database expert yourself, and money is not a problem. (At the time of preparation of this chapter, hourly costs for searching DIALOG ranged from about $45 to $200.)

Online services are constantly striving to become more and more accessible, as their future expansion and competitive edge lies in appealing to a mass, not a specialty, market. DIALOG is developing simple end-user-oriented software, based on icons, to open the service to mass access. The company expects its new products to be available about when this book is published.

Using DIALOG, one can retrieve information on just about any subject or field of knowledge. It also carries the full text of over sixty United States newspapers, most dating back to the 1980s, plus foreign and domestic news wire services. For further information, see your librarian, or contact:

Knight Ridder Information, Inc.
2440 El Camino Real
Mountain View, CA 94040
800-334-2564

LEXIS/NEXIS

LEXIS and NEXIS are second only to DIALOG in size, combining over 350 databases, but they are easier to use. In the past few years, LEXIS/NEXIS developed Windows-based software using a service called Freestyle, which allows for searches in plain English rather than with traditional search commands (Dana Blankenhorn, "Mead Selling Lexis, Nexis," Newsbytes News Network, May 16, 1994).

A customer can have an all-services subscription, or one or a fragment, to permit individuals and organizations to buy only what they need, although this is still at a hefty $500–$700 per month. The effort to attract a popular market has led to the creation of Nexis Express: a student or other researcher can call in with a credit card, and say, "Give me $30 worth of <name that search>." The service uses keywords. The efficient route is first to ask just for citations, then select for more.

You probably can't afford Nexis Express to research the *Roe v. Wade* Supreme Court decision, but you might be able to use it efficiently and economically to find out how to prepare Yorkshire pudding or other less voluminous information. The service offers citations or text or abstracts, and is suitable for such brief searches as recipes, tips on preparing for an interview with a legal firm, or any other very limited search. It is reasonable to expect costs to run from about $30 to $50. Call Nexis Express at 800-843-6476 and make some inquiries. If it looks like your search will cost too much money, go back to the library. Perhaps it is better in many ways for a student to work the stacks, in the end.

LEXIS combines a number of legal databases. It contains federal, state, and local codes and statutes, related legislative material, over seventy law journals, and reports from the American Bar Association. It has indexes of law citations, biographies of about 800,000 lawyers, and information on 50,000 firms. BILLTEXT has the text and Bill Tracking the daily status of bills introduced in the current session of Congress. The same is available for state legislatures.

NEXIS is the master news database, and includes over fifty daily papers across the country. It is the only online service with the *New York Times* in full text, searchable back to 1980. The *Washington Post* is archived back to 1977. NEXIS also includes foreign papers and news wire services. LEXIS and NEXIS have hundreds of thousands of users, not only online but for its CD-ROM version as well. The databases include millions of documents from over 4,000 sources. For further information, contact:

LEXIS/NEXIS PLC
P.O. Box 933
Dayton, OH 45401
800-227-4908

Chapter 5

Secondary Research Using the Internet

Frederick D. King

The Internet is a worldwide network of computer networks that share a common communications protocol, known as TCP/IP. The Internet was developed by the United States Department of Defense as a way of sharing information even in the event of war. Due to the built-in redundancy of its communications paths, information could still travel from one computer to another even if the most direct path between the two were destroyed. Shortly after its development, the research community began to use the Internet to provide access to computers located in remote sites. For example, it was no longer necessary to travel to Stanford University to use one of its computers; you could connect to it any computer that was part of the Internet. In the late 1980s and 1990s, the Internet's popularity began to grow, and currently growth is mushrooming at about 10 percent each month. Nobody knows how many people have access to the Internet, but one estimate puts the figure at over thirty million.

As the Internet grew, people developed a variety of useful applications to make it easier to use. Even more significantly, colleges, universities, government agencies, and other organizations made their resources available, usually without charge, to anyone who wanted to use them. Until recently, commercial activity was prohibited on the Internet, but this restriction has been relaxed, and many companies are making their catalogs available. Some companies will even let you place orders for their products online.

This chapter will discuss two of the most useful ways of getting information from the Internet: via gophers and via browsers that will let you search the newest and most exciting Internet development, the World Wide Web.

GETTING ACCESS TO THE INTERNET

If you are enrolled in a college or university, you probably already have access to the Internet. Most institutions are connected to the Internet, and individual accounts are given to students automatically or are free for the asking. If you are in high school, or if your college does not provide access, you have several alternatives. Some communities have Freenets, which are computer systems available to the public. There may be a one-time registration fee, but, as the name implies, access is generally available without charge. Another option is to get an account on a commercial Internet service provider. There are hundreds, possibly thousands, of Internet providers in the United States, Canada, and elsewhere. Fees charged by these providers can depend on the type of service you choose, the amount of time you spend online, or the amount of data you transfer. Due to the nature of some of the material available over the Internet, some providers limit access to users over the age of eighteen.

Types of Internet Service

The most common type of Internet service is a shell account. You use your desktop computer to connect to the computer where you have your account, and you use that computer as if you were directly connected to it. The connection can be made with a modem over a telephone line, or you can connect through a local area network (LAN) in a computer lab on campus. In either case, you are using the software on the computer you are connected to, not your desktop computer. If you retrieve a file from the Internet, it will be saved on the disk space allocated for your Internet account, and you will then have to transfer it to your own computer.

The other way to use the Internet is with a direct connection. Your desktop computer is connected directly to the Internet, and it has its own Internet address. Many commercial Internet access providers and some colleges and universities offer direct Internet access over a telephone line via a SLIP or PPP connection. (SLIP stands for Serial Line Internet Protocol; PPP stands for Point-to-Point Protocol. They are two slightly different ways of accomplishing the same thing.) With a SLIP/PPP connection, you are limited by the speed of your modem. Most school computer labs have Internet connections through LANs. One advantage of LAN connections is that they are usually much faster than connections over a modem.

WHAT CAN YOU DO ON THE INTERNET?

Although this chapter deals mainly with getting information from gophers and the World Wide Web (discussions of both of these major tools follow this section), there are many other things you can use the Internet for. For more information on these applications, see the suggested readings at the end of the chapter.

Electronic mail. This is still the most widely used Internet application. With electronic mail, or e-mail, you can send messages to people anywhere on the Internet, usually within a few minutes or even seconds.
Discussion lists (or listservs). E-mail provides one-to-one communication; discussion lists provide one-to-many communication. A list is set up to discuss a particular topic, and people subscribe to the list. When you send a message to the list, a computer program known as a list server (the actual name may be listserv, listproc, majordomo, or one of several other programs) automatically sends it to all the subscribers of the list. There are more than 6,500 different discussion lists, with topics ranging from high school physics to Chaucer to vampires.
Usenet. This is not strictly an Internet application, but it is available on many Internet-connected computers. Usenet is a worldwide conferencing system with discussions on almost any topic you can think of and many you can't. Each newsgroup covers a topic; for example, the newsgroup *rec.food.drink.tea* deals with the selection and brewing of tea. Newsgroups have messages, called news articles, which users have contributed. Unlike discussion lists, which send messages to each subscriber, Usenet stores one copy of each Usenet news article on a disk on the service provider's computer. Users read as many articles as they wish (or as they have time for), and the articles are deleted from the system after a certain period of time.

Usenet newsgroups are arranged in hierarchies. The main seven are:

comp   Computer hardware, software, etc.
news   Groups that deal with Usenet administration and an-
        nouncements
rec   Recreation and hobbies
sci   Science
soc   Social and cultural issues
talk   Debates and discussions
misc   Topics that don't fit anywhere else

In addition to these seven, there are several other hierarchies that are widely distributed:

alt   Alternative topics, often of a bizarre and controversial
        nature. Much of the pornography that is causing so much
        concern in the United States is available through the alt
        newsgroups.
bionet Topics of interest to biologists
k12   Topics of interest to elementary and high school students
        and teachers

Other regional, local, and institutional newsgroups may be available only in certain areas.

Telnet. Telnet lets you connect from your computer to another across the Internet and use it as if you were directly connected to that computer. A slightly different version of telnet, developed by IBM, is known as tn3270.

FTP. FTP, or File Transfer Protocol, lets you connect to another computer and copy files from that computer to yours. There are thousands of useful files available in FTP archives all over the world free for the taking, including text files, programs, and graphics. Anonymous FTP allows you to connect to a computer using the user name "anonymous", so you don't have to have an account on that machine.

IRC. Internet Relay Chat provides real-time conferencing over the Internet. It can be useful for talking to people on other continents. IRC is not available on all systems, as it tends to use more resources than most system administrators care to devote to it.

Archie. Archies, or Archive Servers, maintain databases of FTP archives.

If you know the name of the file you are looking for, and you can master the somewhat cryptic searching commands, an archie is a quick way of finding files. If you don't know the file name, gophers and the World Wide Web can be easier to use.

WAIS. Wide Area Information Service is a database-searching tool. It can search the full text of documents in the database and return the results ranked according to their relevancy to your search terms.

WARNING: All of these Internet applications, IRC in particular, can be extremely tempting and addictive. It is quite possible to spend hours and hours on the Internet without realizing it, to the detriment of your studies. Fortunately, there are support groups available to help people kick the Internet habit. Unfortunately, some of them are available only on the Internet.

BURROWING THROUGH THE INTERNET: GOPHERS

The University of Minnesota Computer and Information Services Gopher Consultant service gives this definition for a gopher:

> gopher n. 1. Any of various short-tailed, burrowing mammals of the family of Geomyidae, of North America. 2. (Amer. colloq.) Native or inhabitant of Minnesota: the Gopher State. 3. (Amer. colloq.) One who runs errands, does odd-jobs, fetches or delivers documents for office staff. 4. (computer tech.) Software following a simple protocol for tunneling through a TCP/IP internet.

The Internet gopher was developed in 1991 at the University of Minnesota as a campus-wide information system. Though gopher's popularity has been eclipsed by the World Wide Web, it is still an extremely useful way to search, retrieve, read, and deliver materials from local and remote sites on the Internet. A gopher is organized as a series of menus that leads to other menus, to files, or to a variety of other services. Connections between gophers are seamless, so you can move from one gopher to another without knowing it. You can retrieve material from gophers in the United States, Germany, Australia, and South Africa with equal ease.

How a Gopher Works

A gopher operates on a client-server principle. The client portion of the gopher resides on the computer where you have your Internet account, and the server resides on a computer that could be anywhere on the Internet. When you select a menu item, the client sends a message to the remote gopher telling it to send you that item. This is similar to the process you use when you call a company to request it to send you a catalog. You choose an item in that catalog, and the company sends it to you, just as the gopher requests a file from a remote computer. The difference is that with gopher you don't get a bill at the end of the month.

Connecting to a Gopher

If your Internet system's manager has set up the gopher client conveniently, you may be able to connect to your local gopher simply by typing "gopher" or by typing the name of your institution's gopher at the system prompt. You can connect to a specific gopher by typing "gopher" plus the Internet address of the gopher you want to connect to at your system prompt. For example, to connect to the Library of Congress's gopher, whose address is gopher.loc.gov, you would type "gopher gopher.loc.gov".

If your Internet system doesn't have a gopher client installed on it, you may be able to telnet to a system that allows you to log in anonymously and use the gopher client installed there. In this case, some of the features described here, such as saving files, mailing files, and opening a connection to another gopher, may not be available for security reasons.

An Actual Gopher

Although the methods of navigating through gophers are standardized, the organization of each gopher is different, so it's impossible to tell you exactly what you will find on your local campus gopher. Here is the gopher of Cornish University, an imaginary university located somewhere in the United States:

```
             Internet Gopher Information Client v2.1.1

              Home Gopher server: gopher.cornish.edu

-->   1.    Welcome to the Cornish University Gopher
      2.    About Cornish University
      3.    Applications, Registration, and Financial Aid/
      4.    Academic Departments/
      5.    Course Descriptions and Schedules/
      6.    Cornish University Calendar
      7.    Library/
      8.    Computer Center/
      9.    Student Services/
     10.    CU Phone Directory <CSO>
     11.    Cornish FreeNet <TEL>
     12.    Internet Reference Information/
     13.    Gopher Servers - All over the WORLD!/
     14.    Search the Cornish University Gopher <?>


Press ? for Help, q to Quit                          Page: 1/1
```

Figure 5-1. A typical gopher menu

Gopher menus consist of numbered lines, each of which points to a specific item. The "—>" indicates which line you are currently pointing to. The symbols at the end of a menu item tell you what kind of item it is pointing to. Here are the more common ones:

[a blank space] A file. In most cases, you can read it online, save it in your Internet account space, or, if you are dialing in, download it directly to your computer. Some older versions of the gopher software put a period at the end of a line to indicate a file.

/ A menu. This menu may be on your home system, or it may be on another computer anywhere in the world.

<TEL> A telnet connection to another system. When you select this line, a box will pop up to tell you that you are about to leave the gopher system and connect directly to another computer. Once you leave the gopher system, gopher commands will not work. If you get stuck, you can usually end the telnet connection and return to the gopher by typing ^] (the CTRL key and right bracket). See Figure 5–2 for an example.

<?>   A search. See VERONICA and JUGHEAD below.

<HTML>   A hypertext link. (HTML stands for Hypertext Markup
                 Language.) When you select this line, you will leave
                 the gopher and be transferred to a World Wide Web
                 browser. See the section on the World Wide Web for
                 more information. Not all gopher systems support this
                 type of link.

<CSO>   A search through a name/address directory. Many in-
                 stitutions make their faculty and staff directories avail-
                 able online. When you choose one of these directo-
                 ries, a box will pop up showing what types of informa-
                 tion you can look for. Fill in as much as you can, then
                 hit ENTER. If your search is successful, you will get a
                 page of directory entries that match your search terms.
                 (It's called "CSO" because it was developed at the

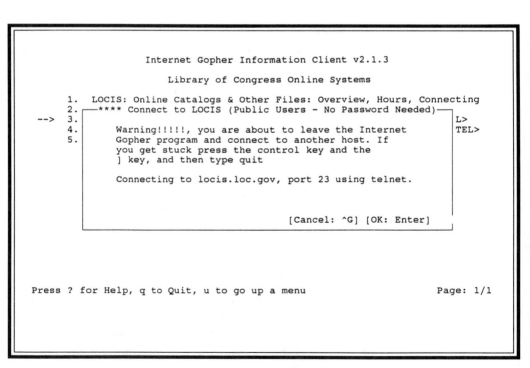

```
               Internet Gopher Information Client v2.1.3

                   Library of Congress Online Systems

     1.  LOCIS: Online Catalogs & Other Files: Overview, Hours, Connecting
     2. ┌─**** Connect to LOCIS (Public Users - No Password Needed)─┐
 --> 3. │                                                           │ L>
     4. │   Warning!!!!!, you are about to leave the Internet       │ TEL>
     5. │   Gopher program and connect to another host. If          │
        │   you get stuck press the control key and the             │
        │   ] key, and then type quit                               │
        │                                                           │
        │   Connecting to locis.loc.gov, port 23 using telnet.      │
        │                                                           │
        │                                                           │
        │                                                           │
        │                                 [Cancel: ^G] [OK: Enter]  │
        └───────────────────────────────────────────────────────────┘




 Press ? for Help, q to Quit, u to go up a menu                  Page: 1/1
```

Figure 5-2. Gophers often help you out of sticky situations with escape
instructions.

Computing Services Office of the University of Illinois, Urbana-Champaign.) See Figure 5–3 for an example.

At the bottom of the screen, you will find some other helpful information:

?   Typing "?" will display a summary of gopher commands.

q   Typing "q" will quit the gopher and prompt you to confirm. If you type "Q" you will quit without being prompted.

1/1   A gopher menu can display eighteen items per page, but there is no limit to the number of items a menu can have. The first number shows what page you are on, the second number is the total number of pages in the menu. If you are on page five of a menu that has seventy-three pages, the bottom right of the screen will show "5/73".

```
                          Cornish University E-mail Directory
 name
 title
 department
 office_location
 office_address
 office_phone
 fax
 pager
 email

[Help: ^-]   [Cancel: ^G]
```

Figure 5–3. It's easy to search Internet directories like this one.

| When a gopher is receiving data, the bottom right corner of the menu will say "Receiving File," and a little twirling wheel will appear. The speed at which the wheel twirls will give you an idea of how fast the information is being retrieved.

Navigating through a Gopher Menu

Seeing a gopher menu isn't much help if you can't move through it. Fortunately, the people who developed the gopher thought of that and provided several ways to navigate through gopher menus. The easiest way is by using the arrow keys. If the arrow keys don't work, you can use letters instead.

Up arrow, k	Move to the previous line
Down arrow, j	Move to the next line
Right arrow, ENTER	Enter/display the current item
Left arrow, u	Exit the current item/go up to the previous menu.
>, space	View the next page of a menu
<, b	View the previous page of a menu
line number	Go to a specific line. For example, to go to line 5, just type "5" and ENTER.
m	Go back to the main menu. (Note: typing "m" when viewing a document will mail the document. It is very easy to confuse the two commands. If you have gone through ten menus to get to the one you want and you accidentally type "m" at a menu instead of a text screen, you will have to retrace your steps to get back.)

Displaying and Saving Text on a Gopher

Once you find a file you are interested in, hit ENTER to display it. Figure 5–4 shows a text file from the Library of Congress.

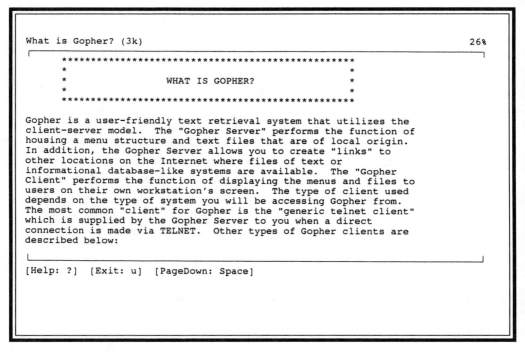

Figure 5–4. This is the first screen of a text file from the Library of Congress's gopher. Choosing a previous menu item, "What is Gopher?" results in this display.

When you display text on a gopher, you can use the following commands to navigate through the text:

Down arrow, space	View next page
Up arrow, b	View previous page
Left arrow, u	Exit the document and go back to the menu
/	Search through the text. This can be useful when you are looking for a particular term in a long document.

The top of the screen will show the title of the document you are displaying, the size of the document (rounded to the nearest 1,000 characters), and the percentage of the document that has been displayed. In this example, the title of the document is "What is Gopher?", the document's size is 3K (approximately 3,000 characters), and 26 percent of the document has been displayed.

At the bottom of the screen are commands to get help, to exit, and to move to the next page.

Saving Text

There are times when it would be helpful to save text to refer to later rather than reading it on the screen. There are several ways to do this. One possibility is to put your monitor face-down on a copier and press the PRINT button, but this is slow and cumbersome. It also doesn't work. You can mail a document to yourself (or to someone else) by typing "m" while displaying the text. A box will pop up asking you the address you wish to send the file to. (See Figure 5–5.) Fill in the address and hit ENTER; the next time you read your e-mail it will be waiting for you. This feature is often unavailable in public-access gophers for security reasons.

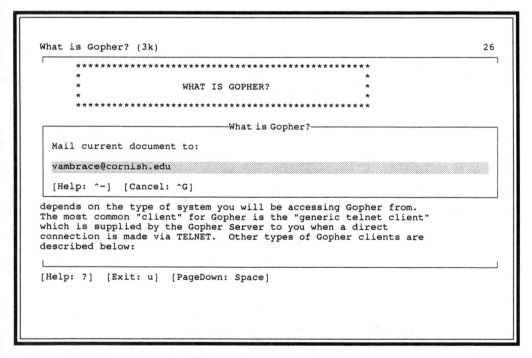

```
What is Gopher? (3k)                                              26

    **************************************************
    *                                                *
    *                    WHAT IS GOPHER?             *
    *                                                *
    **************************************************

                    ─────What is Gopher?─────
    Mail current document to:

    vambrace@cornish.edu

    [Help: ^-]  [Cancel: ^G]

depends on the type of system you will be accessing Gopher from.
The most common "client" for Gopher is the "generic telnet client"
which is supplied by the Gopher Server to you when a direct
connection is made via TELNET.  Other types of Gopher clients are
described below:


[Help: ?]  [Exit: u]  [PageDown: Space]
```

Figure 5–5. You can mail information to yourself or anyone else on the Internet. Pop-up screens like this one make it easy.

You can also save the file in your Internet account. Type "s" and a box will ask you for the file name. A default file name will be provided; if you don't like the one offered, you can use the backspace key or CTRL-U to erase it and then enter one of your own. (See Figure 5–6.) Before you can use the file on your own computer, you will need to transfer it from the computer your Internet account resides on to your computer. Methods of transferring files vary; check with the department that issued your Internet account for instructions. If you are connecting via a public-access gopher, you will not be able to save files since you do not have an account (and disk space) on that computer.

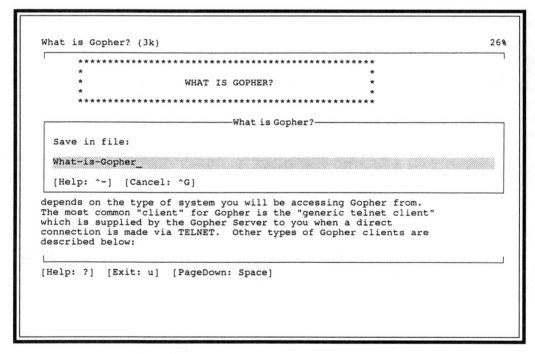

Figure 5–6. Saving a gopher file to your Internet account is also easy: just choose a file name when asked.

The final way to save a gopher file is by downloading it directly to your computer. This method will work only if you are dialing in using a modem and phone line. To download a file, type "D". (That's a capital D, not lower case.) A box will pop up to ask you to select the downloading protocol you wish to use. (See Figure 5-7.) Choose one and hit ENTER. Check the manual of your telecommunications software to see which protocol(s) you can use and how to start the downloading process. Generally, Zmodem is the fastest, followed by Ymodem, Xmodem, then Kermit. ASCII works only with text files and is the least reliable.

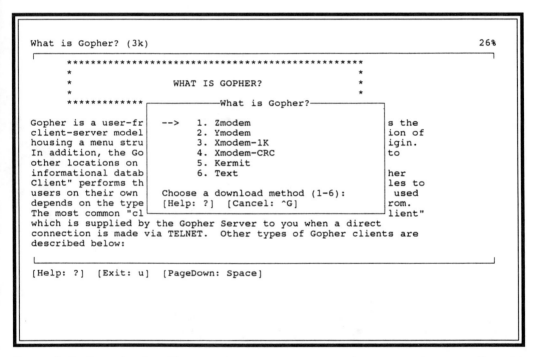

Figure 5–7. Downloading files to disks is a way to save information electronically only for computers using a modem and phone line to connect to the Internet.

Hints for Easy Gophering

Several tricks of the trade can make accessing and using gophers especially productive. Knowing how to create and use bookmarks, locate the authors of gopher files, and jump right to a specific file will all make your research time more productive.

Saving Interesting Menus and Files: Gopher Bookmarks. If you find a menu or file that is especially interesting, you can save it in what is known as a Bookmark file. The addresses of the items are stored in a file in your Internet account, so you can call them up without having to write down how you got there. Follow instructions on your system to do this.

Where Is It? Since gopher connections are seamless, looking at a gopher menu won't necessarily tell you where the menu item is located. By typing "=" when the arrow is pointing at a menu item, you can display the link information. The link information includes the name of the computer the item is stored on (the host), the directory and name of the file (the path), and much more. Some gophers will tell you the name and e-mail address of the gopher administrator, which is useful if you want to contact the file's author.

Going Places: Gopher, Telnet, HTTP, and FTP. If you know the Internet address of a gopher you want to visit, you can enter the address directly by typing "o". A box will pop up to ask you for the address; fill it in and hit ENTER. Newer versions of the gopher software also allow you to use other Internet applications, such as telnet, FTP, and Web browsing directly, without selecting a gopher menu item that points to the application. To start one of these applications, type "w" and enter the complete URL of the item you wish to select. (See page 90 for an explanation of URLs.)

Finding Specific Information in Gopherland

Gophers are very good at displaying text, but if you don't know what menu the text is on, finding it can be a daunting task. The task is even more daunting if you don't know what gopher your text is on. To ameliorate this situation, two gopher searching tools have been developed: VERONICA and JUGHEAD. They both search gophers, but JUGHEAD searches a limited number of gophers and VERONICA searches throughout gopherspace.

VERONICA. VERONICA was developed at the University of Nevada at Reno and it is purported that it stands for Very Easy Rodent-Oriented Netwide Index to Computerized Archives. (Archie, the tool that looks through FTP archives, was developed earlier. Its developers swear that Archie is short for Archive Searcher.) There are a dozen or so VERONICA servers available throughout the world. A VERONICA server periodically searches throughout gopherspace and builds a database of the directories and menu items it finds. This database can then be searched.

Most gophers have a section on "Other Gopher Servers," which includes a menu of VERONICA servers. If you are looking only for gopher menus, choose "Search for Directories." If you are looking for directories and menu items, choose "Search GopherSpace by Title word(s)." When you select a line, a box will pop up to ask you what you wish to search for. Fill in your words, then press ENTER. See Figure 5–8 for an example. It is possible to narrow a VERONICA search using Boolean searching techniques, or to specify that only certain types of files be retrieved. Most VERONICA menus have directions on composing advanced VERONICA searches.

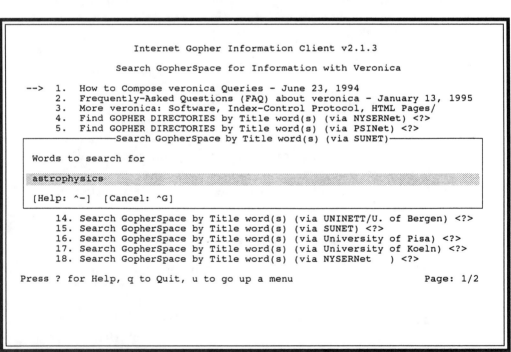

```
                Internet Gopher Information Client v2.1.3

               Search GopherSpace for Information with Veronica

 -->  1.  How to Compose veronica Queries - June 23, 1994
      2.  Frequently-Asked Questions (FAQ) about veronica - January 13, 1995
      3.  More veronica: Software, Index-Control Protocol, HTML Pages/
      4.  Find GOPHER DIRECTORIES by Title word(s) (via NYSERNet) <?>
      5.  Find GOPHER DIRECTORIES by Title word(s) (via PSINet) <?>
  ────────────Search GopherSpace by Title word(s) (via SUNET)────────────

   Words to search for

   astrophysics

   [Help: ^-]  [Cancel: ^G]

     14.  Search GopherSpace by Title word(s) (via UNINETT/U. of Bergen) <?>
     15.  Search GopherSpace by Title word(s) (via SUNET) <?>
     16.  Search GopherSpace by Title word(s) (via University of Pisa) <?>
     17.  Search GopherSpace by Title word(s) (via University of Koeln) <?>
     18.  Search GopherSpace by Title word(s) (via NYSERNet   ) <?>

 Press ? for Help, q to Quit, u to go up a menu                 Page: 1/2
```

Figure 5–8. Searching gopherspace using Veronica is as easy as entering the term you want to search for.

When your search is finished, you will be presented with a custom-made menu what has all the items that match your search. You can connect to any of these items the same way you would with any other gopher menu, but you cannot save the search as a bookmark file. Figure 5–9 shows the result of the search for information on astrophysics.

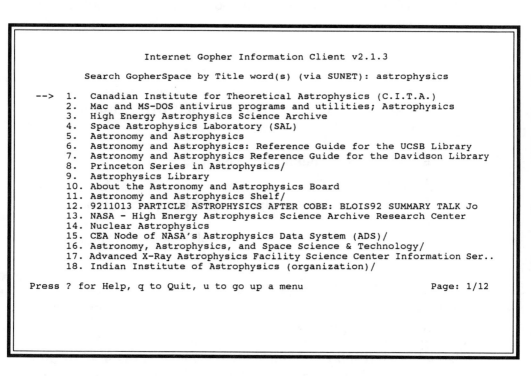

```
                  Internet Gopher Information Client v2.1.3

           Search GopherSpace by Title word(s) (via SUNET): astrophysics

   -->  1.  Canadian Institute for Theoretical Astrophysics (C.I.T.A.)
         2.  Mac and MS-DOS antivirus programs and utilities; Astrophysics
         3.  High Energy Astrophysics Science Archive
         4.  Space Astrophysics Laboratory (SAL)
         5.  Astronomy and Astrophysics
         6.  Astronomy and Astrophysics: Reference Guide for the UCSB Library
         7.  Astronomy and Astrophysics Reference Guide for the Davidson Library
         8.  Princeton Series in Astrophysics/
         9.  Astrophysics Library
        10.  About the Astronomy and Astrophysics Board
        11.  Astronomy and Astrophysics Shelf/
        12.  9211013 PARTICLE ASTROPHYSICS AFTER COBE: BLOIS92 SUMMARY TALK Jo
        13.  NASA - High Energy Astrophysics Science Archive Research Center
        14.  Nuclear Astrophysics
        15.  CEA Node of NASA's Astrophysics Data System (ADS)/
        16.  Astronomy, Astrophysics, and Space Science & Technology/
        17.  Advanced X-Ray Astrophysics Facility Science Center Information Ser..
        18.  Indian Institute of Astrophysics (organization)/

   Press ? for Help, q to Quit, u to go up a menu              Page: 1/12
```

Figure 5–9. This is the first of twelve screens displaying gopher sites with information about astrophysics resulting from the VERONICA search begun in Figure 5–8 above.

Note: Although all VERONICA servers work the same way, they harvest the information at different times, so it is possible to perform the same search on five different VERONICA servers and come up with five different menus. Also since things change so quickly on the Internet, the VERONICA indexes may be out of date and may point to something that no longer exists. And finally, although a VERONICA can search menu names, it cannot search the full text of the documents the menu names are pointing to.

The above VERONICA search shows what happen in an ideal situation. Unfortunately, there are approximately one dozen VERONICA servers in the world, and millions of Internet users, so it is not always possible to have your search done right away. If there are no available connections on the VERONICA server you try, you'll get a message saying that there are too many connections. You can try another server or try your favorite one again later.

JUGHEAD.   It is much easier to perform a successful search using a JUGHEAD. JUGHEAD stands for Jonzy's Universal Gopher Hierarchy Excavation and Display, and is used to index a single gopher or a small group of gophers. The methods for searching a JUGHEAD are the same as for searching a VERONICA.

Problems You May Encounter in Gopherspace

As with most adventures, exploring gopherspace is not always trouble-free. Here are a few errors you may encounter, along with possible causes and solutions.
Connection Refused: The gopher is probably handling as many requests for information as it can, and it is turning away all the others. Try again in a few minutes.
Address Not Found: The gopher probably exists, but your computer can't find it at the moment. Try again later. If you are connecting directly to the gopher using the "gopher gopher.some.node.name" command, check to make sure you have the address exactly right.
Cannot open display or **No display command is mapped to this view!:** This may be a binary (non-text) file. Although a gopher can point to a picture, program, or word processing file, it can't display them on the screen. You can save the file or download it directly to your computer, but you can't look at it.

Stopping a Gopher Transfer

At times, you may get a message that the gopher is connecting, or that you are transferring a file, but nothing seems to be going on. If this happens, you may be transferring a large file, or the link between your computer and the remote computer may be very slow. If you don't want to wait, you can stop the process by typing ^C (holding down the CTRL key while pressing C). On older versions of the gopher client, you will exit the gopher and return to the system prompt. On new versions of gopher, a message will appear at the bottom of the screen asking you if you really want to quit. If you answer "y", you will be returned to the system prompt. If you answer "n", the gopher will stop trying to make the connection, but you will still be in your current menu.

A Few Interesting Gophers

As with anything on the Internet, gophers appear and disappear every day. Now that the World Wide Web is becoming increasingly popular, many gophers are being converted to Web sites. However, several thousand gophers still exist, and they are likely to be around for a while longer. Here are a few starting points.

LC MARVEL

Gopher address: marvel.loc.gov

LC MARVEL stands for Library of Congress Machine Assisted Realization of the Virtual Electronic Library. It has pointers to a wealth of U.S. government resources, ranging from directories of the U.S. Congress to information from dozens of government agencies.

NYSERNet

Gopher address: nysernet.org

NYSERNet is an Internet service provider in New York State. The main menu has pointers to a variety of special collections of Internet resources, some maintained by NYSERNet, some found elsewhere. Among the special collections are a set of resources on breast cancer and the Empire Internet Schoolhouse (resources for K–12 educators and students). This gopher also has pointers to Internet help.

Sailor

Gopher address: sailor.lib.md.us

Sailor is being organized and developed by the state of Maryland to provide public access to Internet resources throughout the state. Sailor has a wide variety of information about state and county government, community information for Maryland counties, and a collection of resources for school-related research topics ranging from biology to economics to religion.

Montgomery Blair High School

Gopher address: goober.mbhs.edu

Montgomery Blair is one of the first high schools to have a gopher. It has pointers to information of use to high school students, and a list of other gophers maintained by high schools throughout the United States.

SunSITE

Gopher address: sunsite.unc.edu

Here is access to software, reference material, music archives, and much more. Of particular interest are the "Internet Dog-Eared Pages," which provide quick reference information.

Carnegie-Mellon University English Server

Gopher address: english-server.hss.cmu.edu

This is an interesting collection of full-text databases covering a variety of subjects including eighteenth-century literature, the plays of Shakespeare, poetry, recipes, and an interview with Beavis and Butt-head.

THE WORLD WIDE WEB

The latest Internet development, and the one that everyone is talking about, is the World Wide Web. The World Wide Web (also known as "WWW" or "the Web") may prove to be the "killer application" that brings the Internet into every home, just as *Lotus 1-2-3* brought a computer into every office. On the other hand, the Web may become the citizens' band radio of the nineties. Only time will tell.

What Is the World Wide Web?

The Web was developed at the European Particle Physics Laboratory in Switzerland as a way to share information among physicists. Tim Berners-Lee, the developer, used hypertext to create documents that were linked together in ways that would allow readers to move from one document to another as they wished.

In a hypertext document, links are embedded throughout the document to lead readers to more information about that link. For example, a document on the United States Congress might have links to the history

of the House and Senate, to biographies of individual senators and representatives, and to articles on the ways lobbyists have influenced the course
of legislation in the past 200 years. Each of these links will give you more
information on a related topic, and the links may themselves have additional links to related topics.

In the World Wide Web, each link may be on a different computer; a
Web page on bird watching in New Jersey may have links to birding docu-
ments on computers in New York, Illinois, Canada, Scotland, and New
Zealand.

The most exciting feature of the World Wide Web is that, unlike gophers, the Web is not limited to displaying text. If you have the right type
of browser, you can display text with headlines, italics, and other features; graphics; sound; and full-motion video. You can even link to a gopher. Some browsers support a function called forms, which allows you
to send information to the Web server. In educational institutions, the
forms function could let you send reference questions and interlibrary
loan requests to the library, or let you register for classes online. Businesses are using forms to let customers fill out orders and submit them
electronically.

The potential of the World Wide Web is just beginning to be realized,
and what it will look like ten years hence is anybody's guess. It is safe to
say, however, that the Web is the most rapidly growing and evolving application on the Internet.

A Few Acronyms and Other Terms

As with most computer applications, the Web comes with a host of acro-
nyms and other cryptic terms to contend with. Here are a few of the
more common ones.

Page: Each Web document is known as a page. A Web page is similar
to one in a book, but it can be of any length and have as many links,
graphics, and paragraphs of text as the designer wants to include.
Most designers of Web pages have one page that is the starting point
to their creations. This top page is usually called the home page.

HTTP: HyperText Transfer Protocol. This is the method that Web
clients and servers use to communicate with each other.

HTML: HyperText Markup Language. Web pages need to have formatting codes to tell the browser where the headlines are, where
the graphics should be placed, and where the links go. These formatting codes are the Hypertext Markup Language, which is simi-

lar to the commands used by typesetting and work processing programs. There are several books and computer programs available to assist Web page designers.

URL: Uniform Resource Locator. This is a standard way of referring to an Internet information source. Although it is most frequently used to refer to Web documents, it can refer to other Internet services as well. A Web URL will have the form "http://www.node.domain/directory/document.html". The "http://" indicates that it is a Web document, the "www.node.domain" is the Internet address of the computer where the document resides, the "/directory/" indicates the location on that particular computer, and "document.html" is the file name of the document. Here are a few examples of Internet information sources as URLs:

http://www.umd.edu The home page of the University of Maryland System

ftp://ftp.ncsa.uiuc.edu The FTP site of the National Center for Supercomputing Applications.

telnet://locis.loc.gov The address of the Library of Congress catalog

gopher://gopher.tc.umn.edu The gopher of the University of Minnesota

Browsing the World Wide Web

Unlike gopher, which has one interface, there exists a multitude of ways to look at the World Wide Web. Most of them are graphical browsers and require special equipment.

Lynx. Lynx was developed at the University of Kansas by Lou Montoulli. It is one of the very few Web browsers that can be run on a dial-up shell account over a slow modem. In fact, all you really need to use Lynx is a terminal capable of emulating a VT100. However, this ease of use comes at a cost. Lynx is text-based, so you won't be able to see all the features, such as graphics, that are making the Web so popular.

In addition to having a gopher, the state of Maryland also has a Web version of Sailor, which has been designed for Lynx and other text-based browsers. Figure 5–10 shows Sailor's home page.

```
                    Sailor's (Maryland's Information Network) Home Port (pl of 2)

    S A I L O R - maryland's online public information network
    _____

    WELCOME TO SAILOR'S HOME PORT
    your gateway to Maryland and beyond
    _____

      * HOME WATERS
          + Maryland State Government
          + Maryland Cities, Counties and Communities
          + Maryland Libraries
          + Maryland Education Resources
          + Other Maryland / Regional Information and Resources

      * TOPICAL CRUISE
          + Computing / Technology / Science
          + Culture / Entertainment / Leisure
          + Economics / Business / Consumer
          + Employment / Career
 -- press space for next page --
    Arrow keys: Up and Down to move. Right to follow a link; Left to go back.
    H)elp O)ptions P)rint G)o M)ain screen Q)uit /=search [delete]=history list
```

Figure 5–10. This is the way Sailor, the State of Maryland's gopher, looks through Lynx, a popular text-based World Wide Web browser.

Navigating through Lynx. The areas in bold indicate hypertext links to other documents. To navigate through the links, use the arrow keys, just as you do with a gopher:

Right arrow or ENTER	Select that link
Left arrow	Go to the previous link
Down arrow	Highlight the next link
Up arrow	Highlight the previous link

The example above shows that we are on page 1 of 2. To get to the next page, hit the space bar or "+". To get to the previous page, type "b" or "-". Some systems will allow you to use the TAB and SHIFT TAB keys to move among horizontal links.

You also have these additional commands:

m   Return to the main screen. You will be prompted be-
            fore you return, so it's harder to use this command acci-
            dentally.
o   Set your options. This will allow you to specify your e-
            mail address, the name of your bookmark file, and a
            variety of other options.
/   Search for text within the document you are currently
            viewing.
n   Search for the next occurrence of the text you found
            using "/".
g   Go to a new location. Enter the full URL (for example,
            "http://www.loc.gov" for the Library of Congress Web
            site) and hit ENTER. This option may not be available
            on all systems.
^R   Reload the current document.
^W   Refresh the screen.
DELETE   History List. Lynx keeps a list of the Web pages you
            have visited during a session. If you want to revisit a
            page, hit DELETE to look at this list.

Saving Text. As with gopher, Lynx allows you to mail, save, or download text. To mail a document, retrieve the document and then type "p"
to display the printing options menu with the following choices (the print
screen itself is shown in Figure 5–11):

```
                                                      Lynx Printing Options
                          PRINTING OPTIONS
      There are 51 lines, or approximately 0 page, to print.
      You have the following print choices
      please select one:

      Save to a local file

      Mail the file to yourself

      Print to the screen




  Commands: Use arrow keys to move, '?' for help, 'q' to quit, '<-' to go back
   Arrow keys: Up and Down to move. Right to follow a link; Left to go back.
   H)elp O)ptions P)rint G)o M)ain screen Q)uit /=search [delete]=history list
```

Figure 5–11. Lynx's print option gives you these easy choices. Notice that Lynx tells you how many lines (and pages if printing will require more than one) printing your file will require.

- Save to a local file: as with gopher, this will save the file in your Internet account. If you want to use it on your own computer, you will have to transfer it from your Internet account.
- Mail the file to yourself: if you select this option, you will be prompted for an e-mail address. Type in the address, then hit ENTER. Lynx does not remember the address, so you will have to enter an address each time you mail a file.
- Print to the screen: almost all communications software will let you save the text scrolling on the screen in a file. This function is called text capture, screen capture, session logging, and a variety of other terms. "Print to the screen" takes advantage of this function. When you select this option, Lynx will pause and prompt you to hit ENTER when you are ready. Turn on the screen capture, hit ENTER, and the file will be displayed. When all the file has been displayed, turn the screen capture off, and the file will be saved on your computer. See your communications software manual for instructions on using screen capture.

Lynx will also let you download a file. To download, highlight the link to the document you wish to download and type "d". Lynx then displays the downloading options page with the following choices:

- Save to disk: this is the same function described above.
- Download using Kermit or Download using Zmodem: these options will download the file directly to your computer.

Warning: Most files available via Lynx have been formatted using HyperText Markup Language (HTML). If you download files, they will contain the HTML formatting commands. If you mail a file to yourself or print to the screen, you will get the text without the codes.

Where Is It? As with gopher, connections between WWW sites are seamless, so you don't always know where you are. By typing "=" at a Lynx screen, you can look at information about the current document (see Figure 5–12 for an example.) This will tell you the name and location (URL) of the document you are currently displaying, and the name and location of the link you currently have highlighted.

```
                                        Information about the current document
                     YOU HAVE REACHED THE INFORMATION PAGE
File that you are currently viewing

   Linkname: Library of Congress World Wide Web Home Page (New version
            05/02/95)
        URL: http://www.loc.gov/
   Owner(s): None
       size: 38 lines
       mode: normal

Link that you currently have selected

   Linkname: Library of Congress
   Filename: http://lcweb.loc.gov/homepage/about.html




Commands: Use arrow keys to move, '?' for help, 'q' to quit, '<-' to go back
   Arrow keys: Up and Down to move. Right to follow a link; Left to go back.
   H)elp O)ptions P)rint G)o M)ain screen Q)uit /=search [delete]=history list
```

Figure 5–12. Lynx will display important information about files upon request.

Bookmarks in Lynx. If you find something interesting in Lynx, you can save the link to it in a bookmark file. When you type "a" Lynx will ask you if you want to save the document or the link to the bookmark file. If you type "d" you will save the document you are currently viewing. Typing "l" will save the highlighted link as a bookmark. Typing "c" will cancel the save. To look at your Lynx bookmarks, type "v". To remove a bookmark entry, highlight the link and type "r".

Problems You May Encounter. **Forbidden.** You will get this error message if you try to view a graphic file. You can download or save it, but as Lynx is text based, it can't display graphics.

Can't access file, Unable to connect to remote host, or **Not found.** These messages indicate that the location or file you are trying to display doesn't exist. The link may have disappeared, the computer you are trying to connect to may be down, or you may have mistyped the address. URLs can get complicated, and it's easy to make a mistake while typing the address. Try again to make sure you have it right.

Stopping a Lynx Transfer. If you are trying to connect to a link that is down, or if you are tired of waiting for a huge file to transfer, you can stop the transfer by typing "z". This will stop what you are trying to do and return you to the current screen. If you type ^C, you will exit Lynx immediately and return to your system prompt.

Graphical Browsers: Text, Sound, Pictures, and More

When most people think about the World Wide Web, they are thinking of graphical browsers. These browsers will display text, sound, pictures, full-motion video, and more. They are easy to navigate through: all you have to do is point to something with your mouse and click a button. Most graphical browsers allow you to save text and graphics, or print them on your local printer.

Graphical browsers are easy and fun to use, but they also have their disadvantages. If you are running one on a PC, you usually need at least a 486 with Windows. You also may need Windows 32-bit extensions, which will allow a 32-bit application to run on a 16-bit operating system.

Unlike gopher and Lynx, which you can use on a dial-up shell account, most graphical browsers require you to have a computer that is directly connected to the Internet. This can be done with a modem over a SLIP or PPP connection, or over a high-speed LAN connection. There are some programs such as TIA (The Internet Adaptor) or Slipknot that will simulate a direct connection on a shell account, but they are still under development.

Finally, the Web can be very slow. If you are using a 14,400-baud modem to view a Web page that has large graphics, it may take minutes for all the files to transfer before you can look at them. One side benefit of browsing the Web is that it teaches patience.

Graphical Web browsers were developed within the past few years, and they are still in their infancy. New browsers appear frequently, and new versions of existing browsers appear even more frequently. The two most popular browsers are Mosaic and Netscape.

Mosaic and Netscape. Mosaic was developed by Marc Andreeson at the National Center for Supercomputing Applications at the University of Illinois, Urbana-Champaign. Although it is copyrighted by the NCSA, it is available without charge for academic, research, and internal business purposes. It takes its name from its ability to draw different types of information from different sources together to present a unified picture. Versions are available for Windows, Mac, and Unix systems. To get the most recent version, FTP to ftp.ncsa.uiuc.edu, then change to the Mosaic directory. If you need Windows 32-bit extensions, it is available here as well. Figure 5-13 shows the Library of Congress's home page as displayed by Mosaic for Windows.

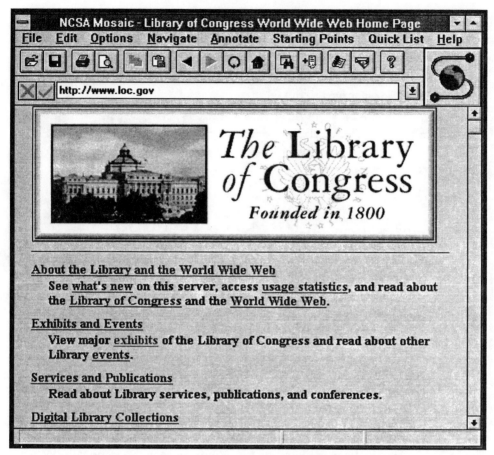

Figure 5–13. This is the way the Library of Congress's home page appears using the Mosaic browser.

As Mosaic's popularity and general usefulness became apparent, Marc Andreeson and other Web developers left the NCSA and formed Netscape Communications Inc. to develop commercial applications of the World Wide Web. They released a browser called Netscape, which is currently the Web's most popular, with an estimated 75 percent share of the market. Like Mosaic, it is available to the academic and research communities without charge, subject to some limitations. The most recent versions for Windows, Mac, and Unix systems are available from ftp.netscape.com. Figure 5–14 shows the Library of Congress's home page as Netscape for Windows sees it.

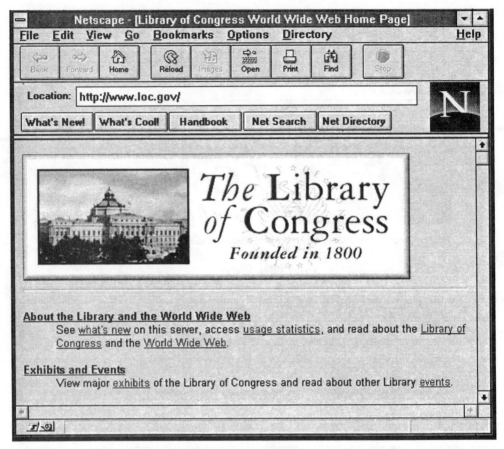

Figure 5–14. This is the way Netscape for Windows sees the same WWW site.

Navigating through Mosaic and Netscape. Both Mosaic and
Netscape have far too many features and capabilities to describe in detail
here. See the suggested readings at the end of this chapter for more information. The descriptions here will give you enough information to get
started using the two browsers and will cover the basics of navigating,
saving and printing files, and creating bookmarks.

As you can see from the examples, although there are slight differences between Mosaic and Netscape, they look very much alike. Since
they were developed by the same teams, this is not altogether surprising.
Links are indicated in each by blue text. To follow a link, move your mouse
to it, then click the mouse button. While your computer is receiving data,
the indicator in the upper right corner of the screen will be active. When
it stops moving, your page has transferred. The bottom line of the screen

will show you the size of the file you are retrieving and how much of it has been transferred. To stop a file transfer in Mosaic, click on the rotating globe. In Netscape, click on the Stop button above the text window. To return to the previous page, click the Back button. When you have viewed a page, the link to that page will be displayed in a different color.

Some Web pages will have links within images. To select a link, move your cursor to the desired portion of the image, then click the mouse button. See Figure 5–15 for an example.

Figure 5–15. The White House's home page has *hot buttons* or *links* for topics like "The First Family" or "Publications." Clicking on any of these will take you to another Web page with information about that topic.

Going to a URL. To go to a specific Web page, you can choose the "File" menu and select "Open Location," or click on the Open button, or type "^O". A dialogue box will appear to ask you for the URL. Type in the entire address, then hit ENTER. (With some versions, you will need to type "http://" plus the address; some versions will accept the address without the http:// prefix.) Figure 5–16 shows an address entered into Netscape. If your browser cannot find the desired page, you may have entered the address incorrectly, or the Web page you are looking for may no longer be there.

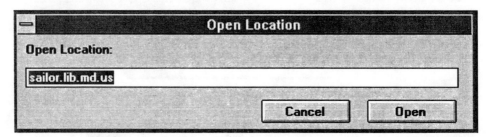

Figure 5–16. Entering a URL in this Netscape window and then clicking on the Open button will take you right to the site you've selected.

Saving and Printing a Page. Both Mosaic and Netscape will allow you to save Web pages on your computer. To save a page, open the "File" menu, then choose "Save". The file you save will include hypertext formatting commands, so you will be able to display it on your browser, but reading it with your word processor may be difficult.

To print a page, open the "File" menu, then choose "Print". The entire page, including graphics, will be sent to your printer. Remember that a Web "page" can be of any length, so it may use up more than one sheet of paper.

Creating Bookmarks. If you see a Web page that you like, you can save its location in a bookmark file, just as you can with gopher and Lynx. Mosaic saves bookmarks in what it calls a Hotlist; to add a location to the hotlist, open the "Navigate" window and select "Add Current to Hotlist", or click on the "Add to Hotlist" button. To browse through your bookmarks, open the "Hotlist Manager" box. In Netscape, open the "Bookmarks" window and choose "Add Bookmark", or type ^A to add a bookmark; choose "View Bookmark" or type ^B to view your bookmark list. Figure 5–17 shows a Netscape bookmark list.

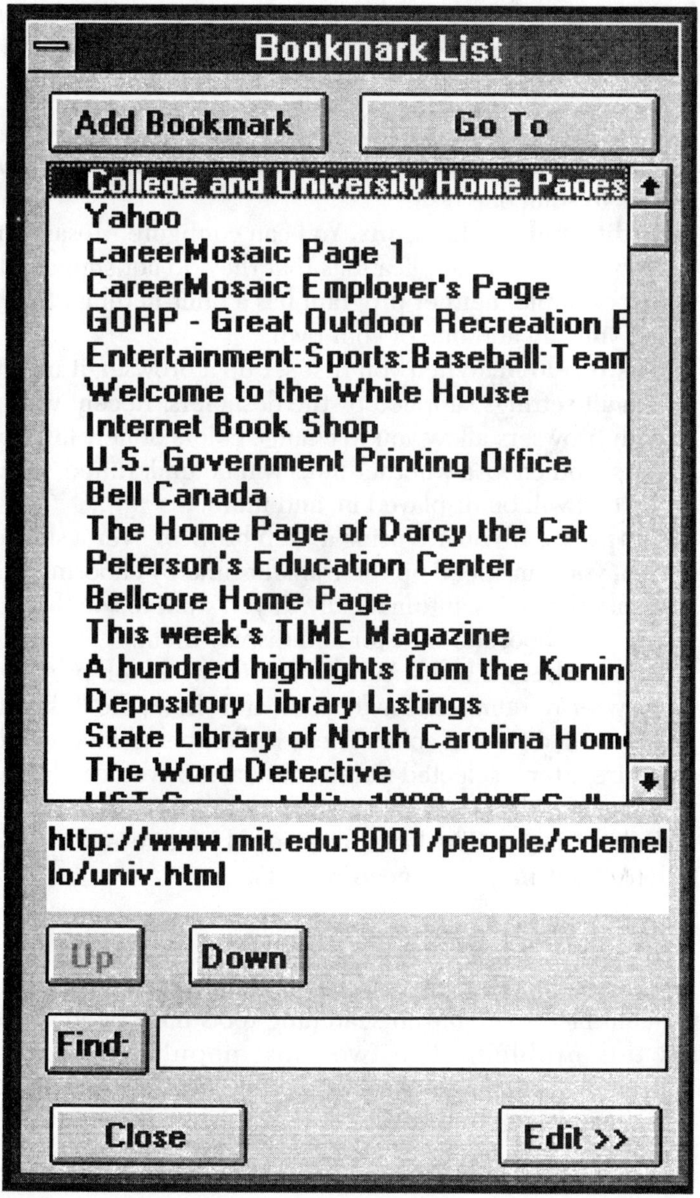

Figure 5–17. This bookmark list was created using the Netscape browser.

Other Features. Both Mosaic and Netscape have many more features than can be described here, and each new release of either brings something new. Here are just a few of the many other features you will find:

- **Mail.** You can mail documents to yourself, or send electronic mail to someone else.
- **Additional applications.** You can configure Mosaic and Netscape to add applications that they do not support directly. For example, neither program has a built-in telnet function, but you can add one of your own.
- **Custom look.** When you first set up a browser, it uses the default settings supplied by the designers. Recent versions of both browsers allow you to change colors of new links or visited links, and choose whether links will be underlined, what fonts the text will be displayed in, and more.
- **Graphics.** If you are using a Web browser over a slow connection, you can speed up the transfer time by choosing not to display graphics automatically. If you want to see the images, you can choose to transfer and display them.
- **Remembered links.** When you display a Web page, your browser remembers the location and shows the link to that page in a different color. These remembered links can be set to expire after a selected number of days, or you can keep them forever.
- **Usenet news.** The latest versions of Mosaic and Netscape have built-in Usenet news readers.

Searching the World Wide Web

With several million Web pages available, finding something on the Web can be daunting. Several Web searching tools have been developed to address this problem. The two most popular are Lycos™ and WebCrawler™. Both have been acquired by commercial companies, but their new owners plan to continue to make their services available without charge.

Lycos™

URL: http://www.lycos.com

This tool was developed at Carnegie-Mellon University and was purchased by CMG Information Services in June 1995. It indexes over four million Web pages.

WebCrawler™

URL: http://www.webcrawler.com

WebCrawler was developed at the University of Washington and was recently purchased by America Online.

Some Interesting Web Sites

With tens of thousands of home pages available throughout the world, and new ones appearing hourly, the "best" Web pages are hard to determine. Here are a few sources of interesting information and links to other sites.

Yahoo

URL: http://www.yahoo.com

If you have just one bookmark in your browser, it should be this one. Yahoo is a listing of over 60,000 Web sites, loosely organized by subject, beginning with Arts, Business and Economics, and Computers and the Internet, and ending with Science, Social Science, and Society and Culture. New links are added daily.

Netscape Corporation's Home Page

URL: http://home.netscape.com/

You can download the latest version of Netscape from here and browse through the other products that Netscape has for sale. This Web page also has links to Web reference materials, listings of new sites, and other Web-related documents.

NCSA's Home Page

URL: http://www.ncsa.uiuc.edu/

The National Center for Supercomputing Applications, the creator of Mosaic, has a Web page as sell. From here, you can download a copy of Mosaic and other software developed by NCSA.

World Wide Web Consortium

URL: http://www.w3.org/

The place to start if you want to learn more about how the Web works and how you can design your own Web pages.

GNN—Global Network Navigator

URL: http://www.gnn.com/

This site was started by O'Reilly & Associates, a leading publisher of Internet books and was acquired by America Online in June 1995. It provides links to Internet resources and commercial Internet services. The Whole Internet Catalog is organized by subject and includes Daily News; Government; Health and Medicine; and Recreation, Sports, and Hobbies.

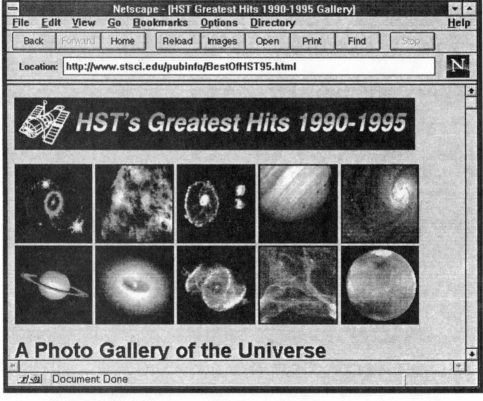

Figure 5–18. A page from the Hubble Space Telescope's Web site.

College and University Home Pages—Alphabetical Listing

URL: http://www.mit.edu:8001/people/cdemello/univ.html

This is a collection of links to colleges and universities throughout the world. If you want to find out more about a particular institution, this would be a good place to start.

Thomas

URL: http://thomas.loc.gov

Thomas is a service of the Library of Congress. It presents the full text of all House and Senate bills and the *Congressional Record.* This is a must for anyone interested in American politics.

Government Printing Office: GPO Access

URL: http://thorplus.lib.purdue.edu:80/gpo/

This is Purdue University's interface to *GPO Access,* a database that provides full-text access to congressional bills, public laws, the *Congressional*

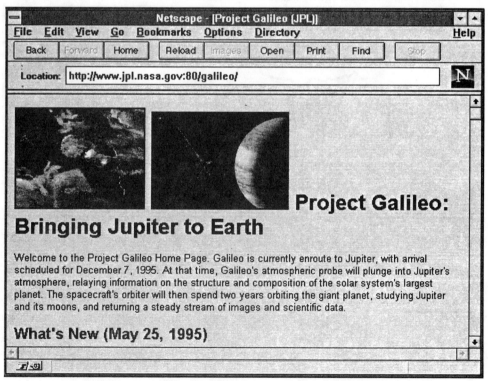

Figure 5–19. The Galileo page at NASA's Jet Propulsion Lab.

Record, and the United States Code. Additional *GPO Access* Web sites
are likely to become available in the near future.

Découverte d'une grotte ornée paléolithique à Vallon-Pont-d'Arc
(Discovery of a Palaeolithic painted cave at Vallon-Pont-d'Arc)

    URL: http://www.culture.fr/culture/gvpda.html

In 1994, archaeologists discovered a group of 20,000-year-old cave paintings in southern France. In order to preserve the paintings, the caves will
not be open to the public, but selected images are available over the
Internet.

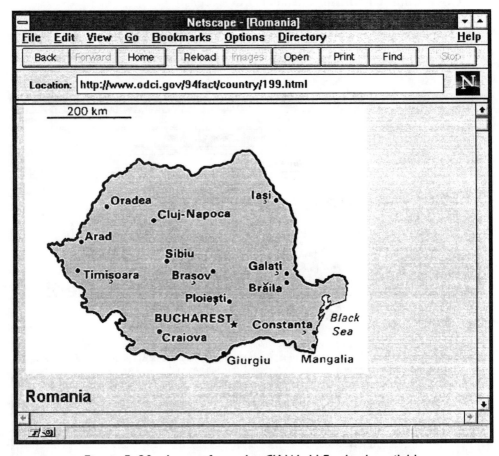

Figure 5–20. A page from the *CIA World Factbook* available
from the CIA's Web site.

ZAK AND KRISTEN SURF THE NET

Remember Zak and Kristen, who were writing their papers on capital punishment and television violence? Here's a hypothetical look at what they might have stumbled across on the Internet while researching their topics.

Zak started out his Internet research by doing a VERONICA search on "capital punishment." He chose "Search Gopherspace by Title Word" because he wanted to do as wide a search as possible. His search produced six pages of references, and from these he found a few items that were of use. Most interesting was a Bureau of Justice *Statistics Bulletin on Capital Punishment 1992*. The search also produced archives of Usenet articles from the newsgroup alt.activism.death-penalty. Zak also searched for "death penalty," which brought up almost 200 entries. As with his previous search, he found a few items of interest, but many of the menu items pointed to sources that were not available. It is likely that the gophers were no longer running and the information VERONICA used to search had not been recently updated.

After looking through gophers, Zak then turned to the Web. He searched the Web using Lycos, which retrieved several hundred Web pages with the words "capital" and "punishment." The Usenet group alt.activism.death-penalty came up again, and Zak used his Web browser to call up and read several of the discussions. He also found a list of Supreme Court decisions by subject on a Web site maintained by Cornell University.

Kristen also searched for her topic using VERONICA, but was not as successful. She tried looking for "television" and "violence" and "children" and turned up nothing. She did the search again, this time just using "television" and "violence" and came up with less than a dozen entries, the most interesting of which was a digest of research on television violence and behavior compiled by ERIC, the Educational Resources Information Center.

Her search using Lycos was much more productive. Among the hundreds of items she turned up were an audio file of an interview with the president of the Children's Television Resource and Education Center, an information sheet produced by the American Academy of Child and Adolescent Psychiatry, a discussion forum sponsored by the Federal Communications Commission on violence, and a press release from the Corporation for Public Broadcasting. Kristen then used Thomas to search the *Congressional Record* for her topic and found speeches, written statements, articles, and proposed legislation. All of these provided good background material that expanded her understanding of her topic.

Both Zak and Kristen found some good supplementary material for their papers, but the Internet cannot yet replace a well-stocked library. Two of the most important resources, books and journal articles, are not yet widely available on the Internet due to copyright restrictions. Furthermore, although the material that Zak and Kristen found came from reliable sources, anyone can put up a Web page with any kind of information. As explained in Chapter 6, just because you've found it doesn't necessarily mean that it's accurate or current. This is true for both Internet and print resources. Consider the source of the information before you rely on it.

FOR FURTHER INFORMATION

Almost any bookstore will have dozens of books about the Internet, all of which will claim to be the only guide you'll ever need. Here are a few to get you started.

Baczewski, Philip, Steve Bang, et al. *The Internet Unleashed*. Indianapolis, IN: Sams Publishing, 1994. $44.95, ISBN 0-672-30466-X, 1387 pp.

December, John, and Neil Randall. *The World Wide Web Unleashed*. Indianapolis, IN: Sams Publishing, 1994. $35.00, ISBN 0-672-30617-4, 1058 pp.

Ellsworth, Jill H. *Education on the Internet: A Hands-on Book of Ideas, Resources, Projects, and Advice*. Indianapolis, IN: Sams Publishing, 1994. $25.00, ISBN 0-672-30595-X, 591 pp. (Intended primarily for teachers, but students will find it useful as well.)

Gilster, Paul. *The Mosaic Navigator: The Essential Guide to the Internet Interface*. New York: John Wiley & Sons, 1995. $16.95, ISBN 0-471-11336-0, 243 pp.

Hahn, Harley, and Rick Stout. *The Internet Complete Reference*. Berkeley, CA: Osborne McGraw-Hill, 1994. $29.95, ISBN 0-07-881980-6, 817 pp.

Harris, Stuart, and Gayle Kidder. *Netscape Quick Tour for Windows: Accessing and Navigating the Internet's World Wide Web*. Chapel Hill, NC: Ventana Press, 1994. $14.95, ISBN 1-56602-244-5, 154 pp.

Krol, Ed. *The Whole Internet User's Guide and Catalog*, 2d ed. Sebastopol, CA: O'Reilly & Associate, 1994. $24.95, ISBN 1-56592-063-5, 547 pp.

Levine, John R., and Carol Baroudi. *The Internet for Dummies*, 2d ed. San Mateo, CA: IDG Books Worldwide, 1994. $19.99, ISBN 1-56884-222-8, 384 pp.

Chapter 6

Examining Sources, Writing, and Revising

Katherine H. Adams and John L. Adams

EXAMINING THE SOURCES

Now that you've gotten information from personal knowledge, primary sources, and secondary resources in a variety of formats, it's time to examine the evidence presented in those sources. As you begin reading the books and articles that you gather, you should carefully evaluate the arguments presented within them. Consider the following questions to judge your sources:

- **The author:** What qualifies the author to speak on the subject? Given the author's credentials and experience, is he or she likely to have a particular bias or be neutral?
- **The source:** Is the publication reputable? Biased? Is it recent or out of date?
- **The audience:** To whom does the author seem to be writing? How does the author deal with the audience's opinions and level of knowledge? Does the author appeal to the readers' emotions?

- **The arguments:** What points is the author trying to make?
- **The evidence:** What evidence is offered in support of each point? Is the evidence sufficient?

TAKING NOTES

After gathering sources and evaluating their worth, you will be ready to begin taking notes, either on note cards (perhaps the larger 4x6-inch size), in a notebook, or on a computer. The following sections will help you to take notes efficiently.

Write Down the Bibliographic Information

When you begin using a source, first record all the bibliographic information (author, title, publisher, volume, pages, etc.), following the documentation form you will be using in the final draft (see the next chapter for more information on documentation). Some people use separate bibliography cards or separate pages in their notebooks for these lists.

When taking notes, clearly identify their source. Start each new card or sheet with the title, author's name, or both (if you are using two works by the same author). Then write down the number of the first page you are using and record each additional page number as you proceed so that you will have the complete citations for your paper.

Using the Computer for Note Taking

As you conduct your research, you might begin using the computer instead of note cards or a notebook. You can open a separate file for bibliography entries, thus creating a bibliography in almost final form. You could then open another file for your notes, separated by numbers or subheadings for different parts of the paper. If you copy a direct quotation into this file, placing quotation marks around it and noting its source, you will not have to recopy it as you draft and revise.

Use a Variety of Note Types

While reading your sources, you may want to take four different kinds of notes—summary, paraphrase, quotation, and personal response—or combinations of them.

Summaries. One helpful type of note summarizes the major assertions and evidence of an entire article or chapter, as in the following example from Kristen summarizing "My Pistol Packing Kids," an article by Jean Marzollo on violent play, film, and television:

Marzollo
Watching violence or playing violent games is actually good for children because it allows them to assume some grown-up control, release their frustrations safely, and play together cooperatively.

Paraphrases. Along with summarizing an entire chapter or article, you may want to record the major ideas from individual paragraphs and sentences. Paraphrasing requires you to think carefully about what the author said and then to recast this content *in your own words and sentence structure.* Make sure that you record the page numbers with these notes.

Kristen, for example, decided to paraphrase the following excerpt from the Marzollo article:

It seems kids want to learn about *both* sides of childhood, not just the mittens and kittens side, full of discovery and nurturing, but also the ghosts and ghouls side, full of dread and helplessness. Watching our children and their friends at play, it is clear to me that the mock violence in their play has a great deal to do with their need to *do* something about the underside of their lives. In order to fight back the witches, giants, and werewolves that menace them at night, they run around in the daytime with toy pistols, toy knives, and toy swords. When I stop to think about their play in these terms, I find I can accept it. (607)

Here is Kristen's paraphrase:

Marzollo
Page 607. Children want to understand the dark and dangerous side of life as well as the innocence of childhood. Violent, imaginative play helps them feel, if only temporarily, as though they can control the larger forces that they don't really understand.

Quotations. You may decide to quote some memorable phrases or sentences directly. (See pp. 118–120 for help with deciding when to use a direct quotation.) Write down every word exactly, mark the quotation with quotation marks so that later you will not mistake it for a paraphrase, and record the page numbers. At this point, you might also make a note about how you could use the quotation in your paper:

Marzollo
Page 607: Violent play comes from children's "need to *do* something about the underside of their lives," about "the ghosts and ghouls side, full of dread and helplessness." These lines are good for stating a common attitude about outside play that this parent also applies to television and movies.

Personal Responses. As you read source materials, you will be changing your own view of the topic. Use a separate card or sheet and write *ME* on it to separate the notes that record your own thinking from summaries, paraphrases, and quotations. Do not wait until later or the idea may be gone.

Marzollo
<u>ME</u>: She bases her argument just on her children and they're both boys—not much real research here. She wants to believe that this violence is all right, a trait she shares with many parents.
For the introduction—playing rowdy games outside is different from television but many parents don't want to acknowledge the difference.

CHOOSING A PRELIMINARY THESIS AND OUTLINE

When you have investigated your topic thoroughly, you will be ready to organize a paper by choosing a thesis and outline.

Deciding on a Tentative Thesis

A *thesis* is a sentence that presents the main idea of the paper, an idea that every fact and detail should support. Although you may alter it after you write a first draft, formulating a thesis now will help you to organize your ideas.
A good thesis has these qualities:

- It states the paper's *topic*.
- It states a *specific opinion* or *attitude* concerning that topic.
- It informs and interests your readers.

When Kristen finished her research on parents' attitudes toward television violence, she realized that she needed a strong thesis to get their attention and state her viewpoint. She first wrote the following sentence:

> Playing cops and robbers games may not be harmful to children, but watching violent television can be.

Kristen then decided on this revision to express her opinions more specifically:

> Playing cops and robbers games may not be harmful to children, but watching violent television each day can make them aggressive, afraid, and less capable of complex thinking.

As Zak investigated thoroughly, he decided that he would argue against capital punishment to his audience of fellow students, who had shown overwhelming support for it in his survey. He wrote the following thesis to state his topic and his opinion concerning it and to address his readers' beliefs:

> Although capital punishment may seem like a fair manner of securing justice, it should be abandoned because it is instead a form of prejudice against the poor of a few states, it doesn't deter crime, and its costs are the highest of any punishment option.

Deciding on an Tentative Outline

After choosing a thesis statement, you should reread your research notes and group them into subtopics. You will then be ready to create a preliminary organization, which may be altered as you write and revise. One structure frequently used for presenting research data is thesis/support:

Introduction
Background information
Thesis statement

1. Consideration of the audience's beliefs on the issue
2. *Your first main point* (beginning the proof of your thesis)
3. *Your second main point* (building on the first point and continuing the proof of the thesis)

4. *Your third main point* (building on the first and second points
    and continuing the proof of the thesis)
         (Continuing with additional points)

Conclusion
    Restatement of the thesis
    Address to the reader
    Statement of implications or a call to action

This structure allows you to address any common misunderstandings about
the issue and then move into your own arguments concerning it. Another
possibility is to refute other viewpoints as you present your own.

    Zak decided to begin with his audience's desire for a punishment to
equal the crime, which they had indicated on their survey. He decided to
then begin his own arguments against the death penalty:

Introduction
    Background information. Survey data on the readers' attitudes
    on capital punishment.
    Thesis statement. Although capital punishment may seem like a
    fair manner of securing justice, it should be abandoned because
    it is instead a form of prejudice against the poor of a few states, it
    doesn't deter crime, and its costs are the highest of any punish-
    ment option.

1. *Consideration of the audience's beliefs on the issue.* The desire
    for justice, which I have shared, is a natural one, but no system
    can offer a punishment to really equal the crimes.

2. *Your first main point.* About the poor of a few states: Only poor
    and minorities, primarily in a few southern states, currently await
    capital punishment.

3. *Your second main point.* About deterrence: Capital punishment
    does not stop crimes from occurring.

4. *Your third main point.* About cost: Capital punishment is the most
    expensive form of punishment.

Conclusion
    Capital punishment should be made illegal nationally.

WRITING THE FIRST DRAFT

Before you start work on a first draft, place your research materials in an order that reflects your outline so that you can find the relevant information easily.

When you begin to write, however, don't feel restricted by this planning. If new ideas come to mind that don't seem to fit with your thesis and outline, write them down anyway to insure that you do not forget them. In fact, you should try to get down every point that may persuade your readers and explain your opinions; you can restructure to incorporate these ideas as you revise. And don't worry about spelling and grammar: they will come later.

Kristen decided when she made her outline to first address her audience's comparison of play and television and then develop her own points on violent behavior, fear, and poor thinking skills. Here is the draft of her second paragraph:

> The effect of television on children has been under investigation for the past few decades. Hundreds of studies and experiments have been conducted which support the theory that television violence has a significant effect on the aggressive tendencies of children. "As early as thirteen years ago," Frost informs, "studies were showing that watching television led to aggressive behavior" (5). Lilian Katz states in one article, "children simply mimic the behavior they observe" (113). One study, involving children who were shown soap operas, reported that the usual game of "mommy and daddy" quickly changed into "you get pregnant, you run away, and you get shot" (Davidson and Pliska 6). This example demonstrates how impressionable young children can be. Another study, conducted for eleven days on preschoolers, had similar results. They viewed several violent cartoons; soon after, a sharp increase of aggression during play was recorded, such as kicking, choking, hitting, and pushing. Most aggressive acts were similar to those from the cartoons (Davidson and Pliska 6).

After she finished, Kristen realized that she had stated her topic and provided data, but she had summarized research findings instead of clearly relating them to her topic.

WORKING WITH SOURCES

As you write your first draft and later as you revise, you will be working on effective and correct use of your sources, in direct quotations, paraphrases, and summaries. Using your notes, you can collect and shape the materials that will support your arguments and convince your readers.

Quoting Sources Effectively

As you work on a first draft, you will need to decide when to quote directly and when to paraphrase your research sources. The key to quoting is not to overdo it. With too many quotations, certainly over two or three on a page, the writing will be choppy, the argument will be unclear, and your own voice will be buried by the others.

You should choose a direct quotation in only two circumstances:

- when you want to provide a sample of a writing style or dialect, or
- when a point or policy is particularly well stated and the exact words are important to your argument.

In the following excerpt on marketing violent television shows, for example, the children's speaking style helps us understand their logic:

> Even though most of the children I interviewed at the video arcade were terribly naive about money and the capitalist system, they seemed keenly aware of the dynamics of consumerist desire. They knew from their own experience that the reported popularity of a commodity and its promotion through commercial tie-ins greatly intensify its desirability to consumers. For example, when asked why they thought Teenage Mutant Ninja Turtles were so popular, one eight-year-old Caucasian boy responded, "Because everybody knows about them and they have lots of stuff," and a ten-year-old Latino boy replied, "They are selling a lot of stuff in stores and usually I buy things like that."
> Marsha Kinder, *Playing with Power: In Movies, Television, and Video Games* (123)

In this second excerpt from the same source, the direct quotation is used to clearly state a company's goals and indicate the attitudes of the spokesman:

The producers of the original TMNT [Teenage Mutant Ninja Turtle] movie took the young core audience for granted and tried to appeal as well to parents and teens (who were probably the readers of the original comic book)—and so they went for a PG rating rather than a G. As Tom Gray, the Los Angeles-based executive in charge of the production company, Golden Harvest, claimed before the film's release: "We purposely skewed this movie for an *older* audience. We know that the kids would come, but we really wanted to make it for the teenage and university level. The script is very, very hip and very timely. We will probably end up with a PG-13 or a PG. . . . A G-rating would kill us." Kinder (132-33)

Choosing Short Quotations. When you have decided that a quotation will be effective because it meets one of these two criteria, choose as short an excerpt as possible to keep the quoted material from overwhelming your own developing argument.

Zak, for example, might want to discuss contradictory attitudes about capital punishment by quoting from this part of Anna Quindlen's essay on her personal responses to mass murderer Ted Bundy:

In a rational, completely cerebral way, I think the killing of one human being as punishment for the killing of another makes no sense and is inherently immoral.

But whenever my response to an important subject is rational and completely cerebral, I know there is something wrong with it—and so it is here. I have always been governed by my gut, and my gut says I am hypocritical about the death penalty. That is, I do not in theory think that Ted Bundy, or others like him, should be put to death. But if my daughter had been the one clubbed to death as she slept in a Tallahassee sorority house, I would with the greatest pleasure kill him myself.

The State of Florida will not permit the parents of Bundy's victims to do that, and, in a way, that is the problem with an emotional response to capital punishment.

(Anna Quindlen, "Death Penalty's False Promise: An Eye for an Eye," pp. 138–39.)

Instead of using the entire excerpt, Zak should quote only the part that is essential to his argument and then continue with his own writing, as in these examples employing MLA documentation (see pp. 121 and 146–150):

Many people, like author Anna Quindlen, find "the killing of one human being as punishment for the killing of another" to be "inherently
immoral" (138).

Quindlen contrasts her "rational, completely cerebral" opposition
to capital punishment with her realization that if her own child were
the victim of a brutal murderer, "I would with the greatest pleasure
kill him myself" (138-39).

Using Ellipses and Brackets with Quotations. By using the ellipsis mark
(…), you can eliminate part of a quoted sentence and thus produce a
shorter quotation that highlights the information essential to your argument. Make sure, though, that the alteration does not distort the meaning of the original work. If some words need to be changed so the quotation will fit into your sentence structure or if you need to add information
to clarify the meaning, you can make those small changes within brackets
([]).

If Zak quoted from the Quindlen essay, for example, he might want to
shorten the final sentence from the excerpt above:

> Even the most avid opponents of capital punishment might change
> their opinions if the murderer had slain one of their family members:
> "But if my daughter had been the one clubbed to death…, I would
> with the greatest pleasure kill him myself" (Quindlen 139).

He might need brackets if he quoted only the final sentence from the
excerpt by itself:

> Although capital punishment may seem to offer justice, families often
> find that it does not fulfill their personal desire for vengeance: "The
> State of Florida will not permit the parents of Bundy's victims to do
> that [kill him themselves], and, in a way, that is the problem with an
> emotional response to capital punishment" (Quindlen 139).

Punctuating Quotations. As the above examples show, *quoted phrases or
words* can be incorporated into your sentences within quotation marks.
No additional punctuation is required.

> Voters must move beyond "an emotional response to capital punish-
> ment" and instead rationally consider the facts about deterrence and
> cost.

When the quotation will be followed in your sentence by a comma or period, place it within the quotation marks:

> Quindlen recognizes that her opinions have been altered by her "three years as a mother," and she admits that any victim's parent might want "something as horrifying as what happened to his child to happen to Ted Bundy."

When you use a *quoted sentence,* join it to the preceding sentence with a colon:

> Anna Quindlen clearly states her reasoned objection to capital punishment: "In a rational, completely cerebral way, I think the killing of one human being as punishment for the killing of another makes no sense and is inherently immoral."

When MLA parenthetical documentation is used at the end of a sentence, the page numbers placed in parentheses come before the period:

> Quindlen believes that capital punishment is not a deterrent to crime because the criminals she has met have "sneered at the justice system" (139).

When you use a longer quotation, one that is more than four lines, indent it ten spaces from the left margin. The quotation should be double spaced, with double spacing also between the quotation and your text. Do not use quotation marks. The MLA documentation should appear outside of the final period:

> Quindlen writes about criminals she has interviewed to explain why capital punishment doesn't deter crime:
>
> > The ones I have met in the course of my professional duties have either sneered at the justice system, where they can exchange one charge for another with more ease than they could return a shirt to a clothing store, or they have simply believed that it is the other guy who will get caught, get convicted, get the stiffest sentence. (139)

Paraphrasing and Summarizing Sources

Since you should choose the direct quotation in only the two situations mentioned above, you will generally use a paraphrase or summary when you discuss ideas and facts from sources.

To summarize or paraphrase, you put the author's ideas *completely into your own words* instead of creating some odd combination of the text's original wording and your own. Consider, for example, this excerpt from an essay on the impact of television and film violence that Kristen wanted to use to support her arguments:

> In panel discussions on this subject, we usually hear claims from TV and movie industry spokespersons that opinion is divided in the medical community. Different conclusions can be drawn from different studies, so the arguments go, and no clear consensus exists. Yet, the American medical establishment is clear—in print—on the subject of just such a consensus. The American Medical Association, the National Institute of Mental Health, the U.S. Surgeon General's Office, the U.S. Centers for Disease Control and the American Psychological Association have concluded that study after study shows a direct causal link between screen violence and violent criminal behavior.
> (David S. Barry, "Growing Up Violent," p. 125.)

If Kristen decided to paraphrase the first sentence of this excerpt, she would need to put it into her own words:

> **Inadequate paraphrase:** In panel discussions on television violence, media spokespersons usually claim that the medical community is divided in its opinion of the topic (125).
> **Adequate paraphrase:** Television and film representatives refuse to admit that medical researchers have identified harmful effects from repeated viewing of violent shows (125).

A good method of paraphrasing is to read the source material, put it down, think through the information, and then write your own version of it.

Introducing Quotations, Paraphrases, and Summaries

One method of introducing the quotation or paraphrase is with a *signal phrase,* which explains to the reader the author's authority or intentions and thus makes the excerpt more meaningful:

Even Anna Quindlen, a liberal columnist who has opposed capital punishment, admits that "my gut says I am hypocritical about the death penalty" (139).

David S. Barry, in an article published by the Center for Media and Values, argues that "study after study shows a direct causal link between screen violence and violent criminal behavior" (125).

When you want the subject matter to remain central, you can also use the *dropped-in quotation* or *paraphrase*, for which the author's name is supplied in the parenthetical documentation:

Many medical organizations, such as the American Medical Association and the Centers for Disease Control, have concluded that television violence causes harm to viewers (Barry 125).

Verb Choices for Introducing Quotations, Paraphrases, and Summaries

When you use a signal phrase to introduce source materials, you might want to choose a more specific verb than *said* to indicate the author's attitude or approach. The following verbs create different meanings that may better represent an author's intentions:

agrees	notes
admits	observes
analyzes	opposes
claims	points out
comments	predicts
concludes	proposes
condemns	relates
considers	reports
describes	sees
disagrees	shows
explains	suggests
insists	thinks
maintains	warns

Avoiding Plagiarism

As you present source materials—quotations, paraphrases, or summaries—you will need to provide documentation for them.

Citations for all three give appropriate credit to the author and enable your readers to locate relevant materials. Correct documentation also requires that all direct quotations, placed in quotation marks, be the author's exact words and that all paraphrases be completely in your own words and sentence structure.

The only exception to the requirement to cite all source materials occurs when you decide that a certain fact is "common knowledge" in the field you are researching. Examples would include the dates of a war or weight of a molecule. If you are in doubt about whether to give credit, however, go ahead and cite the source: no teacher will fault you for being overly careful.

Failing to cite a source, either intentionally or unintentionally, is called *plagiarism* (from the Latin word for "kidnapper"). It is a form of stealing, and thus a punishable offense, since it involves pretending that another person's work is your own.

REVISING

When you have finished a rough draft that incorporates your source materials, your next step is to begin revising, which means "re-seeing" your work from big to small, starting with the thesis and overall structure and then moving to each paragraph and each sentence—to create the best paper that you can.

To begin this step, read your paper carefully and consider the following questions:

1. **Introduction:** Does the beginning involve the reader? Does it state the needed background material?
2. **Thesis:** What is the thesis of the essay? Does it seem clear? Does the body of the paper prove this assertion?
3. **Structure:** Make an outline of the paper's contents. Does the order of points seem appropriate? Should any point be added, moved, or deleted?
4. **Evidence:** Does the essay contain sufficient supporting detail?
5. **Use of source materials:** Are the direct quotations and paraphrases woven into the paper? Are there any direct quotations that

might be removed or shortened? Are all paraphrases correctly done? Are all source materials documented?

6. **Conclusion:** Are the implications of the argument made clear? Is there a call to action or further discussion of the argument's importance?

As Kristen reread her draft, she decided that her thesis was clear and that the structure enabled her to develop each part of her thesis. She had devoted one paragraph to each of her claims: that watching violent television each day makes children aggressive, isolated, and less capable of complex thinking. Within her body paragraphs, however, Kristen realized that she needed better evidence and citation.

As she worked on the second paragraph (for which the first draft is provided on p. 117), she decided that she needed a stronger topic sentence to clearly develop part of her thesis. (A tightened version of her second sentence became that topic sentence.) She also needed more specific explanations of the research studies that would indicate their relationship to her argument. And she decided to move the material on soap operas to the next paragraph since it related to fear instead of aggression. Her revised paragraph is found on pp. 131–132.

When Zak reread his draft, he was pleased with his thesis and overall structure. He decided to work further on developing his paragraphs, especially his conclusion, where he decided to do more than just repeat his criticism of capital punishment and instead discuss moral issues and advocate sentences of life in prison. (His revised essay appears on pp. 137–144.)

Chapter 7

Proofreading and Preparing the Final Copy

Katherine H. Adams and John L. Adams

PROOFREADING

After you finish revising, you will be ready to proofread your paper. At this point, you will need to quit thinking about the ideas and focus on the grammatical correctness of each sentence and the spelling of each word, a task that is easier if you take a break before you begin and allot enough time, perhaps five minutes for each paragraph. Try the following techniques to then turn yourself from writer and reviser into proofreader.

Reading Out Loud

If you read silently, you may think words are there that are not because you will be remembering what you meant to say. Reading the material out loud slowly will help you to focus on what is really there, on each word and each mark of punctuation.

Reading Paragraphs Out of Order

Another helpful technique is to read paragraphs out of order: perhaps the third and then the second or the fifth paragraph. This method will force you to look carefully at the actual words and sentences. You might place a ruler or pencil below each sentence to stop you from reading and thinking ahead.

Using Computerized Spelling and Grammar Checkers

You may also find it helpful to use computerized spelling checkers, but you need to recognize their limitations as well as their strengths.

Instead of noticing all errors, the spelling checker actually points out words that are not in its dictionary. If the computer tells you that a proper noun is "misspelled," it may be correct but missing from the dictionary. Since the spelling checker tells you only whether a word is in its dictionary, it cannot determine whether you have used the wrong word, such as "affect" for "effect" or "there" for "their." After you use a spelling checker, you should proofread for this type of error.

You can check your grammar by using a computerized grammar or style checker. These programs isolate spelling errors, grammatical errors, and poor stylistic choices like passive constructions and overly long sentences. Some also offer explanations of grammar rules.

Like spelling checkers, however, grammar programs have limitations. Even if you agree with the program's analysis of the error, perhaps in subject-verb agreement, you may want to choose another method of correcting it: the checker may suggest changing a subject and predicate verb to the singular, for example, when you meant for them to be plural. Since these checkers do not locate all errors, you will still need to review your sentences carefully.

PRODUCING THE FINAL COPY

When you are ready to produce the final copy, follow these MLA guidelines:

1. Set one-inch margins on the top, bottom, and sides of each page.
2. Number each page, in the upper right corner, one inch from the right and one-half inch from the top. Type your last name before the number. On a word processor, your name and the page number can be placed in the header.

3. You do not need a title page. On the first page of the paper, type your name, your instructor's name, the course number, and the date on separate lines beginning at the left margin one inch from the top. Double-space between each line. Then double-space again and type the title—centered—without underlining it or placing it in quotation marks. Then double-space again and begin typing the text.

4. Indent the first word of each paragraph five spaces from the left; indent block quotations ten spaces.

5. Double-space the entire text, including indented quotations and the list of works cited.

6. Use a separate page, at the end of the paper, for your references. Center the words "Works Cited" at the top of the page. Type the first line of each entry at the left margin; each subsequent line should be indented five spaces. Double-space within and between all entries.

SAMPLE PAPERS

In addition to giving you the above rules for preparing papers, Kristen and Zak's finished, proofread, and polished final papers are presented in the appendix for you to use as models. We've made comments where they have used especially important writing techniques presented earlier in this book.

APPENDIX

Model Paper I

Kristen Hubbard
Dr. Lawrance
English 101
February 17, 1995

Television Violence and Our Children

Children have always made forts and
played war games, without much negative
effect on their behavior toward parents or
friends. These games, in fact, may enable
them to assume some grown-up control, release their frustrations safely, and play
together cooperatively (Marzollo). Many
parents seem to believe that watching violence on television is similar to harmless
"shoot-em-up" games. But parents need to
realize, however, that the games of their
youth are very different from the television experience of today. By the age of
eighteen, American children will have viewed
fifteen to sixteen thousand hours of television while having spent only thirteen
thousand at school and far less playing
outside (Frost 3). During each hour of
viewing, they will see between five and
twenty-five violent acts, with the highest
totals occurring on cartoons and on cable
shows (Barry 124-27). Although playing cops

Hubbard 2

and robbers games may not be harmful to children, watching this amount of violent television each day can make them aggressive, afraid, and less capable of complex thinking. **(1)**

Hundreds of studies and experiments support the conclusion that television violence has a significant effect on the aggressive tendencies of children. As parents, we expect them to mimic many behaviors, such as our manners at a party or treatment of a pet. They will also mimic what they see on a machine they sit in front of during the afternoons and evenings and throughout the weekends (Katz 113). Joe Frost, a British psychologist, contends that "as early as thirteen years ago, studies were showing that watching television led to aggressive behavior" (5). In one such study, preschool children played together, viewed several violent cartoons, and then played again. In the second play sessions, researchers noted a sharp increase in aggressive acts, such as kicking, choking, hitting, and pushing, that were similar to those from the cartoons (Davidson and Pliska 6). Another study of

---

1. Kristen begins by addressing her readers' beliefs and then moves to her thesis. In this paragraph, she summarizes opinions and data with dropped-in paraphrases.

preschoolers judged the postviewing behavior of boys who watched live television
programs with violent content and then played
with toys that encouraged aggressive behavior. On that day and during the next few
weeks, they used the toys to make verbal
and physical attacks that mimicked the shows'
action (Pots, Hutson, and Wright 13-14).
Another study compared a control and a tele-
vision-watching group and found significant differences in their behavior (Josephson). All of these studies leave little
doubt that children imitate what they see.
(2)

Violence on television also affects
children's perception of the actual violence in their environment and thus makes
them afraid. In one study of children watching soap operas, the usual game of "mommy
and daddy" quickly changed into an imita-
tion of soap opera plots, including "you
get shot" (Davidson and Pliska 6). These
children feared violent attacks on their
own families. According to Erin Broussard,
child psychologist and expert on television, children exposed to local news often
fear that robbers or murderers will enter
their homes. Police dramas give them the

---

2. Kristen uses the tag and quotation to present Frost's findings.

impression that children are likely to be
kidnapped or hurt when a crime is committed. Cartoon violence reinforces the notion
that physical attacks are inevitable and
acceptable. All three types of shows can
lead to feelings of isolation and fear and
thus to lowered self-confidence. (3)

Today's violent shows, with their quick
cuts and multiple plot lines, also affect
children's abilities to make connections
between causes and effects, to understand
real human behaviors. The speed of violence, found in videos, drama, cartoons,
and the news, thus cripples the child's
ability to think logically about crisis
events. This "scattered, fragmented form"
trivializes the meaning of each occurrence
(Bogart 255). As Neil Postman contended in
his groundbreaking piece "Future Schlock,"
television viewers become used to seeing
any type of violence, such as that perpetu-
ated in Hitler's concentration camps, as
entertainment and have no interest in a
detailed analysis of the reality. Observation of my own brothers, ages five and seven,
as they watched *Teenage Mutant Ninja Turtles*
confirmed their findings. Every scene seemed
equally entertaining to them, and they especially seemed to enjoy the kicking fights,

---

3 This paragraph includes information from Kristen's interview.

which they reenacted as they watched. When
I asked them why the turtles were being
pursued and attacked, how they could escape, and what they could do to avoid a
repeat attack, they had no answers. They
were simply taking quick scenes as they
occurred without having the time, or perhaps the ability, for reflection. **(4)**

David S. Barry, in an article published
by the Center for Media and Values, argues
that "study after study shows a direct causal
link between screen violence and violent
criminal behavior" (125). He cites research done by the American Medical Association, the U.S. Surgeon General's Office,
and the U.S. Centers for Disease Control to
prove this assertion. We need to heed these
warnings and refuse to surrender our children to that box in the den. Limited viewing, no more than an hour a day, may be
harmless, but children should not be allowed to spend their evenings and weekends
plugged into the set. We cannot wait for
federal legislation, but instead we must
take action ourselves. Just as you might
keep your children from eating only candy
or walking down an interstate, you should
drag them away from the set. **(5)**

---

4. Her observations and discussions with her brothers provided her
data here.
5. Kristen ends with a strong address to her readers.

Works Cited

Barry, David S. "Media's Violence Contributes to Society's Violence." *Mass Media: Opposing Viewpoints*. Ed. William Barbour. San Diego: Greenhaven, 1994. 123-28.

Bogart, Leo. "Advertising Perpetuates Consumerism." *Mass Media: Opposing Viewpoints*. Ed. William Barbour. San Diego: Greenhaven, 1994. 250-55.

Broussard, Erin. Personal Interview. 11 Feb. 1995.

Davidson, Sunny, and Mary Pliska. *Parents Guide for Non-Violent Toy-Buying*. Washington, D.C.: United Methodist Church Board of Society, 1986.

Frost, Joe L. "Influences of Television on Children's Behavior: Implications for War and Peace." International Association for the Child's Right to Play Seminar. London, 29 Dec. 1986. ERIC ED 103 922.

Josephson, Wendy L. "Television Violence and Children's Aggression: Testing the Priming, Social Script, and Disinhibition Predictions." *Journal of Personality and Social Psychology* 53 (1987): 882-90.

Katz, Lilian G. "As They Grow—3 and 4: How TV Violence Affects Kids." *Parents* Jan. 1991: 113.

Marzollo, Jean. "My Pistol Packing Kids."
  The Macmillan Reader. Ed. Judith Nagell,
  John Langan, and Linda McMeniman. 3rd ed.
  New York: Macmillan, 1993. 605-12.

Postman, Neil. "Future Schlock."   *The
  Macmillan Reader.* Ed. Judith Nagell, John
  Langan, and Linda McMeniman. 3rd ed. New
  York: Macmillan, 1993. 247-60.

Pots, Richard, Aletha C. Huston, and John
  C. Wright. "The Effect of Television Form
  and Violent Content on Boys' Attention
  and Social Behavior." *Journal of Experi-
  mental Child Psychology* 41(1986): 1-17.

Model Paper II

Zak Cernoch
Dr. Amato
English 1104
September 12, 1995

A Call for Abolition

At my school, the majority of students, like the majority of Americans, seem to favor capital punishment. A recent survey I conducted indicated that 79 percent of 105 male and female students viewed the death penalty as appropriate for murderers, of one person or of several. A much lower number, under 10 percent, viewed it as appropriate for any other crime. The students' main reason for supporting capital punishment in murder cases was that it offered a penalty equal to the crime. As one student stated, "These killers should get what they dished out." Seventy-five percent also believed that capital punishment was being fairly administered across the nation to combat crime. I agreed with these opinions until I studied the issue more carefully. I now believe that although capital punishment may seem like a fair manner of securing justice, it should be

Cernoch   2

abandoned because it is instead a form of prejudice against the poor of a few states, it doesn't deter crime, and its costs are the highest of any punishment option. **(1)**

Capital punishment might seem like an appropriate penalty if it allowed victims to exact a punishment equal to the crime. Anna Quindlen, a columnist who opposes the death penalty, even admits that any victim's parent might want "something as horrifying as what happened to his child to happen to Ted Bundy," a mass murderer captured after attacking women students at Florida State University (140). But this desire is not fulfilled by the death penalty.   A mass murderer does not endure an equally hideous experience by sitting in the chair and re- ceiving a quick, painless injection. His years living in a clean and safe cell at- tended by lawyers and physicians certainly do not equal what his victims experienced. Since the desire for vengeance cannot actu- ally be served by the justice system, this personal need is not an adequate defense for a punishment that every other Western industrialized nation has abandoned (Zimring 3). **(2)**

---

1. Zak begins with his survey to present the misconceptions he will refute.
2. The quotation from Quindlen states the attitude Zak will discuss in this paragraph.

Since capital punishment is not dis-
pensing the personal style of justice we
seek, we must look at what its purposes and
effects really are. Race, economic status,
education, and state of prosecution have
been the most dominant factors in determin-
ing who will or will not be executed in the
United States. According to Missouri Congressman William L. Clay, Sr., "few 'rich'
persons, if any, have ever gone to the gal-
lows. The ranks of the condemned are heavily
populated by poor whites—those condemned
for reasons other than their specific crimes—
and by minorities who are damned by socio-
economic pressures" (7). Former governor
of California Edmund (Pat) Brown points out
that "dozens of reputable studies show that
the race of the victim as well as that of
the criminal plays a vital part in deciding
whether a murderer lives or dies" (160). A
1980 survey by William Bowers and Glenn
Pierce concluded that, in Georgia, blacks
who killed whites were eighty-four times
more likely to receive the death penalty
than blacks who killed blacks; in Texas,
blacks who killed whites were eighty-four
times more likely to receive death sentences. The study also found that killers
of black victims, whether they were white
or black themselves, were punished by death

less than one-tenth as often as killers of
white victims.   Another study found that
"there has been a systematic, differential
practice of imposing the death penalty on
blacks and, most particularly, when the
defendants are black and their victims are
white" (Zimring 35).   These prejudicial
decisions, also, occur in only a few states.
From 1977 to 1992, of 188 executions, 145
occurred in Texas, Florida, Louisiana, Georgia, and Virginia (*World Almanac* 217). **(3)**

Besides being an unfair alternative lev-
ied against the few, capital punishment is
a very costly alternative. The actual cost
of execution includes the price for defense
and prosecuting attorneys, court costs,
operating costs of super maximum security
units, and a share of top-level prison officials' time. David Lester, a professor of
psychology and criminal justice, says that
other costs processed through many different agencies must be considered as well,
especially those from the extended appeals
process, which may take ten years or more.
These court costs must be absorbed by different levels of government because, as Congressman Clay explains, "less than 1% of

---

3. Data from a Congressman, a governor, researchers, and an almanac are combined here to define how capital punishment affects
the poor.

Cernoch 5

over 2000 inmates sitting on death row had legal counsel paid for by private funds. Over 99% of those awaiting execution are indigents who were represented by public defenders or counsel appointed by the courts" (145–46). Governor Brown points to a study in 1982 that "had the total of a trial and appeals pegged at 1.8 million dollars—more than twice what it would cost to keep even the youngest and hungriest prisoner alive and behind bars for the rest of his life" (161). Using more recent figures, Sister Helen Prejean states that one prisoner on death row costs Louisiana over three million dollars (171). **(4)**

For these exorbitant costs, states are not getting a deterrent to crime. "Deterrence" refers to a circumstance in which an individual refrains from an act because he or she perceives a risk of punishment for the act and fears that punishment. When the death penalty was instituted, one of the strongest supporting factors was that it would stop many people from killing others. Sociologists say that this perception is wrong. Clay concluded that

---

4. Here Zak uses quotations and paraphrases to discuss reasons for the high cost of capital punishment and then to provide specific estimates.

in practice, three-fourths of
all murders involve family members or close acquaintances who
are killed out of anger or pas-
sion.   Clearly the threat of
execution has little or no effect on such spontaneous, un-
premeditated acts. Moreover,
premeditated murders are committed by people who clearly
do not expect to be appre-
hended, and who will state so
when and if they are captured.
(9-10)

Clay also insists that common sense
should tell us that "three hundred years of
American experimentation with capital punishment has not decreased the number of
capital crimes one whit" (69). Statistics
really prove the opposite, that states with
no death penalty have a lower average murder rate than those states with the death
penalty, 4.75 per 100,000 population as
compared to 6.8 per 100,000 (Brown 156).
(5)
Because of its real costs and ineffec-
tiveness, the death penalty should be abol-

---

5. The indented quotation explains why executions do not affect
the murder rate.

Cernoch   7

ished in the United States. As a nation, we
proclaim that we are the most advanced,
most respected, most fair, and most civi-
lized in the entire world. Having capital
punishment is a direct contradiction of this
proclamation. A much better alternative is
life imprisonment without possibility of
parole, which protects society from the
offender and exacts a long, hard punishment, at a much lower cost. **(6)**

---

6. The final paragraph provides Zak's alternative solution.

Works Cited

Brown,   Edmund, and Dick Adler.   *Public Justice, Private Mercy.*   New York: Weidenfield, 1989.

Clay, William L.   *To Kill or Not to Kill.* San Bernandino, CA: Borgo, 1990.

Lester, David.   *The Death Penalty: Issues and Answers.*   Springfield, IL: Thomas, 1987.

Prejean, Helen.   *Dead Man Walking.*   New York: Random, 1983.

Quindlen, Anna.   "Death Penalty's False Promise: An Eye for an Eye." *Elements of Argument.* Ed. Annette T. Rottenberg. New York: St. Martin's, 1990.

The World Almanac and Book of Facts. Mahwah, N.J.: Funk and Wagnalls, 1995.

Zimring, Franklin E., and Gordon Hawkins. *Capital Punishment and the American Agenda.* New York: Cambridge, 1986.

Chapter 8

Citing Print and Electronic Sources

Renée M. Prestegard

WHAT ARE CITATIONS?

In doing research for your term paper you will gather information from print sources (such as books, journals, or newspapers) and from electronic sources (such as CD-ROMs or the Internet). You will use the facts, ideas, and opinions stated by others in order to support your own thesis statement. At times you will quote exact phrases or sentences that particularly support the topic of your paper.

As you draw on these sources you must acknowledge the origins of the information or quotations you incorporate into your paper. Presenting information gleaned from other sources as if it is your own is called plagiarism. You will avoid plagiarism by creating citations within the text of your paper, giving credit to the author for borrowed quotations, ideas, and opinions. Citations refer to an alphabetical list of works cited, included at the end of your paper. The list of works cited enables the reader of your paper locate your source materials.

STANDARD CITATION FORMATS

Many scholarly disciplines have developed style manuals for the literature of the field. Two widely used citation formats are those illustrated in
the style manuals of the Modern Language Association of America (*MLA
Handbook for Writers of Research Papers*, fourth edition) and the American Psychological Association (*Publication Manual of the American Psychological Association*, fourth edition). There are many other style manuals, such as *The Chicago Manual of Style,* fourteenth edition, which is
widely used in many fields. This comprehensive manual covers all aspects of manuscript preparation and printing. In preparing your paper,
you should use the style specified in your assignment. If you're not sure
which one to use, check with your instructor. The majority of this chapter
concentrates on the MLA and APA styles since they are the most commonly used.

Citations in both the MLA style and the APA style are brief, and appear in parentheses at the end of the sentence or paragraph containing
information gleaned from source materials. In an MLA citation, include
the last name of the author of your source, and the page number(s) on
which you found the information. For an APA citation add the date the
source was published, and add the abbreviation "p." before the page
number(s). If there is no author (or no page number, as is possible with
electronic sources), use the elements available. Compare the same citation in MLA style to the APA style:

MLA
In the jazz community, the emphasis on individuality and freedom of
expression in creating music coexists with the interdependence of play-
ers within a group (Berliner 418).

APA
In the jazz community, the emphasis on individuality and freedom of
expression in creating music coexists with the interdependence of play-
ers within a group (Berliner, 1994, p. 418).

These brief citations within the text of the paper refer to a bibliography
(a list of references) included at the end of the paper. The bibliography
lists all cited works, alphabetized by author's name or by title if there is
no author. For more information about Berliner's work, the reader can
turn to the bibliography and find the author's name, the title of the source,

and the publication information. The majority of this chapter will concentrate on formats to use in your list of cited sources.

A bibliography entry in the MLA style includes the author's full name (last name first), the title of the work (with all important words capitalized), the city in which the work was published (abbreviated if necessary), an abbreviated form of the publisher's name, and the date of publication. The first line of an entry in the MLA style is flush with the page's left margin, and subsequent lines are indented:

Berliner, Paul F. *Thinking in Jazz: The Infinite Art of Improvisation*. Chicago: University of Chicago Press, 1994.

An entry in the APA style begins with the author's last name, first initial, and the date of publication enclosed in parentheses. Only the first word of the title is capitalized, although the first word of any subtitle, appearing after a colon, is also capitalized. Finally, the city of publication and the full name of the publisher are included. The first line of the entry is indented, and subsequent lines are flush with the left margin:

Berliner, P. (1994). *Thinking in jazz: The infinite art of improvisation*. Chicago: University of Chicago Press.

Though citations and bibliographies prepared following other style manuals convey the same information, the formats vary. For example, an in-text citation following *The Chicago Manual of Style* would look like an MLA citation, but the bibliography entry combines elements of both the MLA and APA styles:

Berliner, Paul. 1994. *Thinking in jazz: The infinite art of improvisation*. Chicago: University of Chicago Press.

MLA and APA Basic Entries

MLA Basic Entry: Books

Format:

Author's Name. *Title of the Book*. City of Publication: Publisher, Year of publication.

Example:

Schell, Orville. *Discos and Democracy: China in the Throes of Reform.*
New York: Pantheon, 1988.

MLA Basic Entry: Periodicals

Format:

Author's Name. "Title of the Article." *Periodical Title* Date Month Year:
page numbers.

Example:

Cooper, Marc. "The N.R.A. Takes Cover in the G.O.P." *Nation* 19 June
1995: 877+.

APA Basic Entry: Books

Format:

Author, I. (Year). *Title of the book.* City of Publication: Publisher.

Example:

Camp, H. C. (1994). *Iron in her soul: Elizabeth Gurley Flynn and
the American left.* Pullman, WA: WSU Press.

APA Basic Entry: Periodicals

Format:

Author, I. (Year, Month Date). Title of the article. *Name of Publication, Vol*, page numbers.

Example:

James-Catalano, C. (1995, April). Cyberlibrarian. *Internet World,
6*, 92–93.

HOW TO CITE ELECTRONIC INFORMATION

Print sources are not going to be obsolete any time soon, but you can now
find electronic versions of hundreds of bibliographic databases, as well as
entire books, encyclopedias, and other reference sources. Your campus

library probably owns many CD-ROM titles, and provides access to online computer services and the Internet.

Parenthetical citations in the text of your paper to electronic resources will follow the same style explained above. The entries in the list of works cited, however, will contain more information for electronic resources than entries for print resources include. When citing materials gleaned from electronic sources, you will add a statement about the publication medium; for example, CD-ROM or online. In addition, you will add information about the vendor or provider of the electronic database. Finally, in the case of online databases, you will add information about the electronic path you took to find the information.

Online databases, especially on the Internet, are increasing and changing on a daily basis. The path you follow to locate materials may, in fact, not work the next time you try to find the materials, but it is important that you include an "availability" statement for the online works you use and cite. Part of the purpose of listing the works cited is to enable the reader to locate the materials. Although it is possible that the databases you use via online services will change locations, or disappear altogether at some point, it is important to document how you were able to locate and use the information at the time you were conducting research.

MLA Style for Citing Electronic Materials

The latest editions of both the MLA and APA style manuals now address formats for citing electronic information. The 1995 edition of the *MLA Handbook for Writers of Research Papers* divides electronic publications into portable databases and online databases. Portable databases are distributed on CD-ROMs, diskettes, and magnetic tape. You need special computer equipment in order to read and use these electronic publications. Most college and university libraries have several portable databases (usually CD-ROM) in their collections, as well as the equipment necessary to search for information in these databases.

In order to access online databases, you use a computer to connect to the databases through a service or telecommunications network. Although not portable, online databases are often more current. Online information can be revised and updated on a monthly, weekly, or even daily basis. There is a charge, based on connect time and the amount of information retrieved, for searching online databases accessed through computer services such as DIALOG, BRS, Dow Jones News Retrieval, and LEXIS. Because of this, your campus library may not allow you to search databases available through these online services yourself, but will provide this service for students and faculty. Most campuses, however, are now providing students and faculty with accounts for computer networks such as the Internet.

Portable Databases

MLA Basic Entry Formats: Periodically Published Databases on CD-ROM. For databases that are periodically published on CD-ROM and have a print counterpart, MLA recommends including the following elements in each cited work:

Author's Name. "Title of the Article." *Periodical Title* Date Month Year [of print publication]: page numbers. *Title of the Database*. CD-ROM. Name of the Vendor. Electronic publication date.

For databases that are periodically published on CD-ROM but have no print counterpart, MLA recommends the following style:

Author's Name. "Title of the Part of the Work Accessed." Date Month Year [if given]. *Title of the Database*. CD-ROM. Name of the Vendor. Electronic publication date.

Examples: CD-ROM with Print Counterpart.

"European Recovery Aids U.S. Oil Firms' Revenues." *European Chemical News* 30 Jan. 1995: 14. *F & S Index Plus Text*. CD-ROM. SilverPlatter. 1995.

Harler, Curt. "What's Your Firm's Plan for Dealing with Techno-phobes?" *Communications News* March 1995: 4. *Computer Select*. CD-ROM. Information Access Company. 1995.

Kolata, Gina. "Men and Women Use Brain Differently, Study Discovers." *New York Times* 16 Feb. 1995, late ed.: A1. *New York Times Ondisc*. CD-ROM. UMI-ProQuest. 1994.

Purdum, Todd S. "Clinton Asks Rise in Minimum Wage." *New York Times* 4 Feb. 1995, late ed.: A1. *New York Times Ondisc*. CD-ROM. UMI-ProQuest. 1994.

Whitaker, Nancy. "Whole Language and Music Education." *Music Educators Journal* July 1994: 24–28. *ERIC*. CD-ROM. SilverPlatter. 1995.

Examples: CD-ROM with No Print Counterpart.

"Minnesota Mining & Manufacturing Co." *Compact Disclosure*. CD-ROM. Disclosure. 1995.

National Trade Databank. CD-ROM. U.S. Dept. of Commerce. Jan. 1995.

MLA Basic Entry Formats: Nonperiodical Databases on CD-ROM, Diskette, or Magnetic Tape.

Cite nonperiodical electronic publications on CD-ROMs, as well as diskette and magnetic tape publications, as you would cite a book, but add information about the publication medium. If the part of the work you are citing is a section of the larger database, enclose it in quotation marks. If the part of the work you are citing is a work in itself, underline it.

Author's Name. "Title of the Part of the Work Accessed." *Title of the Database*. Edition, Release, or Version. Publication medium [CD-ROM, Diskette, or Magnetic tape]. City of Publication: Publisher, Year of publication.

Author's Name. *Title of the Part of the Work Accessed. Title of the Database*. Edition, Release, or Version. Publication medium [CD-ROM, Diskette, or Magnetic tape]. City of Publication: Publisher, Year of publication.

Examples: Nonperiodical Databases on CD-ROM, Diskette, or Magnetic Tape.

"Aaron Rents, Inc." *U.S. Equities OnFloppy*. Ver. 4.1. Diskette. Chicago: Morningstar, 1995.

County Agriculture. Magnetic tape. Bala Cynwyd: WEFA Group, 1993.

"Harp." *Microsoft Musical Instruments*. CD-ROM. Redmond, WA: Microsoft, 1992.

Herman, Mary Ann. "Folk Dance." *Academic American Encyclopedia*. Ver. 4.0. CD-ROM. Danbury, CT: Grolier, 1991.

"Kaufmann." *Mutual Funds OnFloppy*. Ver. 1.0. Diskette. Chicago: Morningstar, 1995.

Louis Armstrong: A Multimedia Record. CD-ROM. Chicago: Compton's, 1994.

"Louisa May Alcott." *Academic American Encyclopedia.* Ver. 4.0. CD-ROM. Danbury, CT: Grolier, 1991.

"Vesterheim Norwegian American Museum." *American Library Directory.* Magnetic tape. New Providence, NJ: Bowker, 1993.

World Almanac and Book of Facts. Microsoft Bookshelf. Ver. 6.0. CD-ROM. Redmond, WA: Microsoft, 1994.

Online Databases. As we discussed above, online databases can be accessed through computer services or through telecommunications networks. Because online databases are revised and updated more frequently than portable databases, it is important to include in your citation the date you (or the librarian assisting you) conducted your search.

MLA Basic Entry Formats: Computer Services: Databases with a Print Counterpart. MLA recommends including the following elements for databases searched through services, such as DIALOG, BRS, or LEXIS, that have a print counterpart:

Author's Name. "Title of the Article." *Periodical Title* Date Month Year [of print publication]: page numbers. *Title of the Database.* Online. Name of the Computer Service. Date Month Year [of access].

Examples: Computer Services: Databases with a Print Counterpart.

Atwong, Catherine T., Irene L. Lange, and Kahlid M. Dubas. "An Analysis of Japanese Direct Investments in the U.S." *American Business Review* June 1995: 41–46. *ABI/INFORM.* Online. DIALOG. 15 June 1995.

Goodstein, Laurie. "Churches May Not Be Able to Patch Welfare Cuts." *Washington Post* 22 Feb. 1995, final ed.: A1. *Washington Post Online.* Online. DIALOG. 22 Mar. 1995.

McKay, Jim. "Information Revolution: Librarians Adapt to On-line World." *Pittsburgh Post-Gazette* 16 Apr. 1995: D1. *Pittsburgh Post-Gazette*. Online. DIALOG. 26 Apr. 1995.

If you cannot find some of the information required for the MLA style of citation, use what is available:

"An Analysis of Japanese Direct investments in the U.S." *American Business Review* June 1995: 41–46. *ABI/INFORM*. Online. 15 June 1995.

MLA Basic Entry Formats: Computer Services: Databases with No Print Counterpart. If the online database has no print counterpart, MLA recommends including the following:

Author's Name. "Title of the Material of the Work Accessed." Date Month Year [of material; if given]. *Title of the Database*. Online. Name of the Computer Service. Date Month Year [of access].

Examples: Computer Services: Databases with No Print Counterpart.

"IBM Stock: Quotes from 19 May 1995 to 24 May 1995." *Dow Jones Historical Quotes*. Online. Dow Jones News Retrieval. 26 May 1995.

"Top 25 Mutual Funds: 16 June 1995 to 22 June 1995." *Mutual Funds Performance Report*. Online. Dow Jones News Retrieval. 22 June 1995.

MLA Basic Entry Format: Computer Networks: Periodicals. Electronic databases, as well as the full text of electronic journals and books, are now available through networks such as the Internet and BITNET. MLA recommends including the following elements when searching periodically published materials such as electronic journals, newsletters, and conferences:

Author's Name. "Title of the Article or Document." *Title of the Journal, Newsletter, or Conference* Vol. or issue number. (Date Month Year): number of pages, or n. pag. ["no pagination"]. Online. Name of the Computer Network. Date Month Year [of access]. Available [method used to search the network]: electronic address In: Path used to access materials

According the *MLA Handbook*, including an availability statement is optional when citing materials gleaned from computer networks; however, without it your reader would not be able to try to locate the materials cited. As discussed above, information on computer networks, especially on the Internet, is continually revised and updated, and it is possible that the address and/or directory path you used to locate the materials will change. This is why it is important to include the date of access in your citation, and to document the method you used at that time to locate the materials.

Begin the availability statement by indicating whether you reached the electronic database via an FTP or telnet session or by using search mechanisms such as gopher or the World Wide Web. Finally, include the electronic address you used and the path of the directories or menus through which you found the materials.

Examples: Computer Networks: Periodicals.

Brady, Diane. "As the World Learns: American Students Need to Be Better Educated If They Are to Compete in the Global Economy." *Mother Jones* (Sept./Oct. 1993): n. pag. Online. Internet. 20 June 1995. Available World Wide Web: http://www.mojones.com In: Mother Jones Magazine/1993 Issues/September-October/As The World Learns

Browner, Jessica A. "Wrong Side of the River: London's Disreputable South Bank in the Sixteenth and Seventeenth Century." *Essays in History* 36 (1994): 35–72. Online. Internet. 15 June 1995. Available Gopher: minerva.acc.virginia.edu In: Library Services/Electronic Journals/Essays in History/1994/Wrong Side of the River

Rezmierski, Virginia. "Computers, Pornography, and Conflicting Rights." *Educom Review* 30.2 (Mar./Apr. 1995): n. pag. Online. Internet. 1 June 1995. Available Gopher: gopher.lib.virginia.edu In: Educom Review 1995/March-April/Computers, Pornography, and Conflicting Rights

Sengers, Phoebe. "Madness and Automation: On Institutionalization." *Postmodern Culture* 5.3 (May 1995): n. pag. Online. Internet. 16 June 1995. Available Gopher: jefferson.village.virginia.edu In: Publications of Institute/Postmodern Culture/V5 N3, May 1995

MLA Basic Entry Formats: Computer Networks: Electronic Texts. If you are citing an electronic version of a printed text, include the following:

Author's Name. *Title of the Text.* City of Publication: Publisher, Year of publication. Online. Name of the Repository of the Electronic Text. Name of the Computer Network. Date Month Year [of access]. Available [method used to search the network]: electronic address In: Path used to access materials

Examples: Computer Networks: Electronic Texts.

Copyright Basics. Online. LC Marvel. Internet. 9 May 1995. Available Gopher: marvel.loc.gov In: Copyright/Copyright Basics (Circular 1)

Kentridge, Robert W. *Symbols, Neurons and Soap-Bubbles and the Neural Computation Underlying Cognition.* Online. Princeton University. Internet. 16 June 1995. Available FTP: princeton.edu In: pub/harnad/Computation/Kentridge_Neural.Computation

"Minnesota." *1990 USA Census Information.* Online. U.S. Bureau of the Census. Internet. 19 June 1995. Available Gopher: spinaltap.micro.edu In: Ebooks/By Title/1990 USA Census Information

Okerson, Ann, ed. *Directory of Electronic Journals, Newsletters & Academic Lists.* Washington, DC: ARL, 1994. Online. Association of Research Libraries. Internet. 29 May 1995. Available Gopher: arl.cni.org In: Scholarly Communication/Directory of Electronic Journals, Newsletters & Academic Lists

APA Style for Citing Electronic Materials

The 1994 edition of the *Publication Manual of the American Psychological Association* does not examine electronic citations as thoroughly as the *MLA Handbook*; however, APA does also divide electronic publications into CD-ROM (portable) and online (computer services and networks) databases. The basic styles are based on those developed by Xia Li and Nancy B. Crane in their publication *Electronic Style: A Guide to Citing Electronic Information* (1993).

The major difference between APA and MLA, aside from differences in spacing and punctuation, is that APA does not list the availability statement as optional. APA in fact makes a distinction in the availability statement as to whether materials cited are abstracts or from a full-text database. If you are citing information gleaned from an electronic abstract of an article or book, then precede your availability statement with "Abstract from:" If you are citing materials from a full-text database, precede the availability statement with "Available:"

CD-ROMS

APA Basic Entry Formats: CD-ROMs.

Author, I. (date). Title of article [CD-ROM]. *Title of journal, vol.,* pages. Abstract from: Name of Vendor File: Name of File Item: item number

Author, I. (date). Title of article [CD-ROM]. *Title of journal, vol.,* pages. Available: Name of Vendor File: Name of File Item: item number

APA Examples: CD-ROMs.

Exxon is latest to bat with polymer booster [CD-ROM]. (1995, March 6). *Chemical Marketing Reporter,* 3. Available: SilverPlatter File: F & S Index Plus Text Item: 4429099

Netto, A. (1995, March 30). Eye opener: Magazine editor tests the limits of press freedom [CD-ROM]. *Far Eastern Economic Review, 158,* 78. Abstract from: Information Access Company File: Expanded Academic Index Item: A16811620

Nicolson, G. L. (1995, Feb. 22). Doxycycline treatment and Desert Storm [CD-ROM]. *JAMA, 273,* 618–619. Abstract from: SilverPlatter File: Medline Item: 95147321

Pfiffner, P. (1995, June). Point, shoot, click: Apple, Kodak digital cameras aim for mainstream [CD-ROM]. *MacUser,* 26. Available: Information Access Company File: Computer Select Item: 16861602

Pollack, A. (1994, April 26). Jeep is giving Chrysler a success story in Japan [CD-ROM]. *New York Times,* D1. Abstract from: UMI File: Newspaper Abstracts Item: 02954313

R & D budgets bounce back as optimism prevails [CD-ROM]. (1995, March 8). *Chemical Week,* 26. Available: SilverPlatter File: F & S Index Plus Text Item: 4429660

Online

APA *Basic Entry Formats: Online.*

Author, I. (date). Title of article. *Name of Periodical* [Online], *vol.* Abstract from: Name of Vendor File: Name of File Item: item number

Author, I. (date). Title of chapter. In *Title of full work* [On-line]. Available FTP: address Directory: Name of directory File: Name of file

Author, I., Author, I., & Author, I. (date). *Title of full work* [On-line]. Available: Name of Vendor File: Name of File Item: item number

Author, I., Author, I., & Author, I. (date). *Title of full work* [On-line]. Available Gopher: address Directory: Name of directory File: Name of file

APA *Examples: Online.*

Atwong, C. T., Lange, I. L., & Dubas, K. M. (1995, June). An analysis of Japanese direct investments in the U.S. [On-line]. *American Business Review,* 41-46. Available: DIALOG File: ABI/IN-FORM Item: 01023004

Clinton, W. (1993, January). *Clinton's Inaugural Address* [Online]. Available Gopher: spinaltap.micro.edu Directory: Ebooks/By Title File: Clinton's Inaugural Address

Kentridge, R. W. (1995, June 16). *Symbols, neurons and soap-bubble and the neural computation underlying cognition* [On-line]. Available FTP: princeton.edu Directory: pub/harnad/Computation File: Kentridge_Neural.Computation

McKay, J. (1995, April 16). Information revolution: Librarians adapt to on-line world [On-line]. *Pittsburgh Post-Gazette*, D1. Available: DIALOG File: Pittsburgh Post-Gazette Item: 08107104

Sengers, P. (1995, May). Madness and Automation: On Institutionalization. *Postmodern Culture* [On-line] 5. Available Gopher: jefferson.village.virginia.edu Directory: Publications of Institute/Postmodern Culture File: V5 N3, May 1995

BIBLIOGRAPHY

The Chicago Manual of Style. 14th ed. Chicago: University of Chicago Press, 1993.

Gibaldi, Joseph. *MLA Handbook for Writers of Research Papers*. 4th ed. New York: MLA, 1995.

Li, Xia, and Nancy B. Crane. *Electronic Style: A Guide to Citing Electronic Information*. Westport, CT: Meckler, 1993

Publication Manual of the American Psychological Association. 4th ed. Washington, DC: APA, 1994.

About the Authors

John L. Adams is an instructor of English at Loyola University/New Orleans. He has published articles in *Journal of Teaching Writing, Rhetoric Society Quarterly, The Writing Instructor*, and other journals. His books include *The Accomplished Writer* and *Teaching Advanced Composition: Why and How*. His co-authored chapter on using creative writing pedagogies in writing labs recently appeared in *Intersections: Theory-Practice in the Writing Center*.

Katherine H. Adams is a professor of English at Loyola University/New Orleans. She has published articles in *College Composition and Communication, Rhetoric Review, Teaching English in the Two-Year College, The Writing Instructor*, and other journals. Her books include *The Accomplished Writer, The Easy Access Handbook: A Writer's Guide and Reference* (with Michael L. Keene), *A History of Professional Writing Instruction in American Colleges*, and *Teaching Advanced Composition: Why and How*. She is currently finishing a book on writing instruction during the Progressive era.

Carol Felstein, a consultant and freelance writer for the past ten years, is a former New York City Deputy Commisioner of Housing who at one time oversaw the largest automated municipal heat complaint system in the country. She finds signing onto Prodigy or AOL and "cruising the Net" to be far better entertaininment. Ms. Felstein also writes fiction.

Charles Harmon is Director of Acquisitions & Development for Neal-Schuman Publishers, Inc. He holds a B.A. in English from High Point College and a master's degree in library science from the University of North Carolina-Greensboro. He has taught high school English, worked in school and public libraries, and most recently served as Director of the Headquarters Library for the American Library Association.

Frederick D. King received his master's degree in library science from the Catholic University of America. He has worked for the American Library Association, the Library of Congress, and the University of Maryland University College. While at the American Library Association, he started and edited ALAWON, *the ALA Washington Office Newsline*, an electronic newsletter covering federal library issues. He has written on a variety of topics, including federal legislation dealing with privacy issues, public access to the Internet, and how to choose an Internet service provider. He lives in Maryland with his books, computers, and tropical fish.

Renée Prestegard is Associate Director and Librarian at the American Library Association's (ALA's) Library and Research Center in Chicago, Illinois. She has previously held the positions of Reference Librarian and Acting Director of ALA's Library and Information Center. She received her B.A. in English from Luther College in Decorah, Iowa, and her M.A. in Library and Information Studies from the University of Wisconsin-Madison.

Sarah Sheehan-Harris has a B.A. in English and a master's degree in library and information science from the Catholic University of America. She is the Reference Librarian for the University of Maryland University College. She has previously worked at Frostburg State University and the University of Maryland-Baltimore County.

Mark Vecchio's poetry has been published on both sides of the Atlantic (U.S. and England), and he is a recipient of the T. S. Eliot Poetry Award. He holds an M.F.A. in poetry from the City University of New York, Brooklyn College, and a D.Univ. (first class) in classics from the University of Kent at Canterbury. Mr. Vecchio teaches English at Simon's Rock College of Bard, and gives private creative writing workshops and tutorials in Amherst, Massachusetts.

Index

Other Titles of Interest

THE INTERNET COMPENDIUM: GUIDES TO RESOURCES BY SUBJECT

By Louis Rosenfeld, Joseph Janes, and Martha Vander Kolk

This unique series compiled by a team from the acclaimed University of Michigan Internet Clearinghouse, provides direct location access to a virtual mall of over 10,000 Internet addresses in hundreds of subjects.

Subject Guides to Humanities Resources
1-55570-218-X. 1995.
8 1/2 x 11. 368 pp. $75.00.

Subject Guides to Health and Science Resources
1-55570-219-8. 1995.
8 1/2 x 11. 529 pp. $75.00.

Subject Guides to Social Sciences, Business and Law Resources
1-55570-220-1. 1995.
8 1/2 x 11. 424 pp. $75.00.

Buy all three subject guides for $175
1-55570-188-4.

"While indexing the ever-changing environment of the Internet may seem an impossible job, this series makes an excellent start and will be valuable on the reference shelf for both librarians and patrons." *Library Journal*

FINDING GOVERNMENT INFORMATION ON THE INTERNET:

A How-To-Do-It Manual
Edited by John Maxymuk

Keep this indispensable step-by-step manual handy to quickly locate and deliver the latest local, state, federal, and international government information to your library, as well as augment your collection.

1-55570-228-7. 1995. 8 1/2 x 11.
264 pp. $39.95.

THE GOOD DETECTIVE'S GUIDE TO LIBRARY RESEARCH

By Barbara J. Brown

Here is an up-to-date, user-friendly guide designed to make students and other researchers comfortable with library materials including encyclopedias, almanacs, atlases, dictionaries, CD-ROMs, and online systems. Readers will also learn the ins-and-outs of classification systems, bibliographies, indexes, government documents, bibliographical sources, and more!

1-55570-197-3. 1995. 6 x 9.
200 pp. $24.95.

Publication dates, prices, and number of pages for new titles may be estimates and are subject to change.

To order or request further information, contact:

Neal-Schuman Publishers
100 Varick Street, New York, NY 10013
212-925-8650
or fax toll free—1-800-584-2414